THE AMERICAN KENNEL CLUB'S
Meet the
Dachshund™

The Responsible Dog Owner's Handbook

AKC's
Meet the Breeds
Series

PRESS

Irvine, California
A Division of
I-5 Publishing, LLC

An Official Publication of The American

AMERICAN
KENNEL CLUB

Brought to you by The American Kennel Club and The Dachshund Club of America.

Vice President, Chief Content Officer: June Kikuchi
Vice President, Kennel Club Books: Andrew DePrisco
Lead Editor: Karen Julian
Art Director: Cindy Kassebaum
Production Manager: Laurie Panaggio
Production Supervisor: Jessica Jaensch
Production Coordinator: Leah Rosalez

Photographs by: Gina Cioli/I-5 Studio: 90; Dwight Dyke, Blackhawk Productions: 110-111, 119; Laurie Meehan Elmer: 3, 8, 42, 72, 78, 79, 101, 107; Cheryl Ertelt: 12, 18-19, 43, 70-71; Isabelle Francais: 9, 28, 33, 35, 56, 65, 77, 80-81, 92; Fiona Green: 44, 49, 54, 74, 76, 82, 84, 86, 94, 95, 96, 97, 102, 106; Daniel Johnson/www.foxhillphoto.com: 4 (bottom), 53, 62; Paulette Johnson/ www.foxhillphoto.com: 29, 88-89, 120; Mark Raycroft: title page, 4 (top and center right), 6-7, 11, 15, 16, 17, 21, 22-23, 24, 27, 30-31, 34, 37, 40, 47, 55, 58, 60, 66, 69, 85, 91, 98-99, 112, 116, 121; Shutterstock: 13, 14, 32, 36, 59, 67, 87, 104, 109, 117, 124; Sporthorse Photography: 4 (center left), 38, 45, 50-51, 52, 64, 68, 83

I-5 Press
Division of I-5 Publishing, LLC
3 Burroughs, Irvine, CA 92618

Library of Congress Cataloging-in-Publication Data

The American Kennel Club's meet the dachshund : the responsible dog owner's handbook.
     pages cm. -- (AKC's meet the breeds series)
 "An Official Publication of the AKC."
 Includes bibliographical references and index.
 ISBN 978-1-937049-99-7
 1. Dachshunds. I. American Kennel Club. II. Title: Meet the dachshund.
 SF429.D25 A65
 636.753'8--dc23
                        2012031230

Printed and bound in the United States
17 16 15 14 13   1 2 3 4 5 6 7 8 9 10

Meet Your New Dog

Welcome to *Meet the Dachshund*. Whether you're a long-time Dachshund owner, or you've just gotten your first puppy, we wish you a lifetime of happiness and enjoyment with your new pet.

In this book, you'll learn about the history of the breed; receive tips on feeding, grooming, and training; and learn about all the fun you can have with your dog. The American Kennel Club and I-5 Press hope that this book serves as a useful guide on the lifelong journey you'll take with your canine companion.

Owned and cherished by millions across America, Dachshunds make wonderful companions and also enjoy taking part in a variety of dog sports, including Conformation (dog shows), Obedience, AKC Rally®, and Agility.

Thousands of Dachshunds have also earned the Canine Good Citizen® certification by demonstrating their good manners at home and in the community. We hope that you and your Dachshund will become involved in AKC events, too! Learn how to get involved or find a training club in your area at www.akc.org.

We encourage you to connect with other Dachshund owners on Facebook (www.facebook .com/americankennelclub) and Twitter (@akcdoglovers). Also visit the website for the Dachshund Club of America (www.dachshund-clubofamerica.org), the national parent club for the Dachshund, to learn about the breed from reputable exhibitors and breeders.

Enjoy *Meet the Dachshund*!

Sincerely,

Dennis B. Sprung
AKC President and CEO

6

30

60

40

Contents

The Dachshund Mystique

The outline of the Dachshund—an elongated body on very short legs—is instantly recognizable and cannot be mistaken for any other canine. The very definition of "form follows function," Dachshunds were designed to tunnel underground in pursuit of their quarry. For all his sweetness and charisma, the Dachshund is fierce and fearless when working. The Doxie is a spirited, independent thinker, and you would be too if you were burrowing through a hole after

Dachshunds are busy dogs with playful personalities, requiring owners who will give them constructive ways to occupy themselves.

an angry badger fighting for its life! Although the breed has been described as somewhat stubborn, it is in fact one of the brightest hounds out there, as demonstrated by the Dachshund's success in field trials, tracking work, and more.

Dachshunds come in two sizes: Standards weigh from 16–32 pounds and stand 8–9 inches high at the shoulder; Miniatures weigh 11 pounds or less and

stand 5–6 inches high at the shoulder. They also come in three different coat types: longhaired, smooth, and wirehaired.

Dachshunds love to play, but the games have to be to their liking. The bright Doxie is unlikely to share a toy with you, fetch a ball or a Frisbee, or repeat the same game more than twice. Smart dogs, like smart kids, bore easily, so mix up the games to keep your dog interested. A fast, curious Doxie mind needs constant stimulation, or the dog will find alternative ways to occupy himself.

Dachshund owners must have a good sense of humor. As loyal and bright as any dog, Dachshunds have their own way of thinking. The Doxie's determination to get a job done translates to persistence and perseverance when hunting in the field.

WHO'S THE BOSS?

Loyal, intuitive, and strong-minded, Dachshunds can be obedient and rewarding companions. Most Doxie owners contend that their dogs can read minds and are able to pick up on their owners' body language. If your Dachshund thinks that you don't know how to solve a problem or that you're lacking in the "top dog" department, he will step in and take over.

You have to always be in control of your dog and his surroundings. Make it clear to your dog that you are the boss, not him. Dachshunds are sensitive dogs, so never be unkind or harsh when giving corrections, but use an authoritative tone of voice to get your dog's attention and respect.

When the puppy comes home, begin his education right away. Don't be afraid to be the "alpha dog" on day one: your Doxie wants and needs a leader.

Did You Know?

Dachshund is German for "badger dog," after the quarry the breed was designed to hunt. The name Dachshund was first cited in print in 1685, and prior to that these dogs were called "burrow dogs," "earthdogs," "badger creepers," and *bibarhunds,* meaning "beaver dogs." The Dachshund is known around the world as *Teckel, Dachel,* and *Dachsel.* Today the breed has nicknames as well, including "Doxie," "Dachsie," and "Weiner dog."

But that doesn't mean you have to be a no-fun boss all the time. Play with your Dachshund and be his appreciative audience as he acts the clown with his creative puppy antics. Dachshunds love attention, and nothing will make your puppy happier than interacting with his number-one human.

This breed loves people and, if well socialized, will revel in the attention of the whole family. That said, Dachshunds are the epitome of one-person dogs: they bond extremely closely with the one person whom they view as their human. They like to stick close by their person, offering nearly constant companionship, protection, and plenty of unsolicited advice. The clever Dachshund is never without an answer: no quandary, puzzle, or problem can stump a Dachshund.

Any dog that's bred to badger badgers is one tough little guy, and the Dachshund doesn't need coddling. But he does need to be looked after, for his own good. This applies to all aspects of his care, including diet, exercise, and health.

MEMBERS OF THE DOXIE'S HOUSEHOLD

Most Dachshunds like kids, but not all kids. This breed is not the best choice for families with toddlers or small children. Dachshunds naturally relate to little people but prefer the company of well-behaved older children who are smart enough to treat the Dachshund with gentleness and respect. When socialized with children, Dachshunds can be very accepting and protective of their young friends. Dachshunds have little patience for ill-behaved or abusive youngsters who tease them, disregard them, or overwhelm them. The breed likes kind and friendly attention.

Invest time socializing your Dachshund with children, and instruct your children on the proper way to handle a Dachshund. Doxies don't take kindly to the rough antics of kids—children should never sit on a Dachshund, attempt to mount the dog's back, or otherwise harm the dog. Be forewarned that a Dachshund mistreated by youngsters will not hesitate to protect himself from a child who relentlessly taunts him. Always supervise your Dachshund when he's interacting with children, no matter how well behaved or experienced with dogs the young people may be.

Doxies are gregarious canines that get along nicely with other dogs, provided they are introduced properly in a neutral setting. The dogs will have to work out who will be the alpha dog, which may take a little growling, sniffing, barking, and shifting of ears and tails. Generally speaking, dogs of the same sex don't get along as easily as opposite-sex pairs do.

If you have a family cat, your Dachshund will likely accept her in time. The two animals must be carefully introduced, and the owner must make it clear to the Dachshund that the cat is a member of the family. Most felines are as fearless as Dachshunds, which can lead to disagreements punctuated by hissing, snarling, and screeching. In time, canine and feline will either accept each other or dutifully ignore each other. Other small mammals in the house are an entirely different story. Your Dachshund will be utterly perplexed and agitated by your decision to house "prey," a.k.a. rabbits, rats, hamsters, and other "varmints" that he is instinctually drawn to hunt and chase. There is nothing you can do to convince the Dachshund otherwise: prey is prey.

A VOCAL HOUND

Hounds will be hounds, and they were born to bark. Dachshunds may not howl and bay as much as foxhounds and coonhounds, but once they grow into their voices, they're pretty talented talkers. You certainly cannot judge a Dachshund's bark by his height: with a deep chest and resonant resolve, the Standard Dachshund sounds like a much larger (and taller!) dog. The Miniature's bark isn't as deep and can sound a bit squawky, which many owners dislike—and as luck would have it, Miniatures tend to be more talkative. Protective of their family and home turf, Dachshunds make reliable watchdogs that will attentively sound an alarm when something or someone is amiss.

A Doxie's education and socialization must begin in puppyhood.

A WEINER WITH A WAIST

The Dachshund's bloodlines may trace to Germany, but its ever-expanding waistline has its roots in the USA! Dachshunds love to eat! Obesity in America has become a national epidemic, and not just with Dachshunds. Thankfully, Americans have become more health-conscious, paying more attention to calorie, carb, and fat content than ever before. We have to do the same for our grub-loving Doxies. It's much easier for your Dachshund to diet than it is for you. Your Dachshund can't get off the couch at night to fetch that pint of Häagen-Dazs from the freezer!

Your Dachshund's waistline isn't a matter of vanity, but of continued good health. Given the unusual structure of the breed, the Dachshund is susceptible to

The curious and alert Dachshund revels in the sights—and especially the scents—of the great outdoors.

intervertebral disk disease, which causes slipped or herniated disks in the back. Additional weight on the dog's frame places unnecessary stress on the vertebra and can lead to lameness and eventual paralysis. Exercise is an important part of any dog's health regimen, and Dachshunds are no exception, but owners must be sure to limit their Dachshunds' jumping and stair climbing. You'll never keep your dog from jumping entirely, but you can try to discourage it when you're present. Eighteen-wheelers aren't built for high jumps, so keep your Dachshund from leaping off furniture, patios, or your lap, and only allow your dog to climb stairs on leash. Dashing down the stairs is decidedly bad for the Dachshund's spinal cord.

UNIQUE COATS, UNIQUE PERSONALITIES

All Dachshunds must be friendly, lively, and bold. The individual personality of every dog varies, and wirehaired, smooth, and longhaired Dachshunds tend to have different temperaments. Historians point to crosses in the breed's past to

Responsible Pet Ownership

AMERICAN KENNEL CLUB™

Getting a dog is exciting, but it's also a huge responsibility. That's why it's important to educate yourself on all that is involved in being a good pet owner. As a part of the Canine Good Citizen® test, the AKC has a "Responsible Dog Owner's Pledge," which states:

I will be responsible for my dog's health needs.

☐ I will provide routine veterinary care, including checkups and vaccines.

☐ I will offer adequate nutrition through proper diet and clean water at all times.

☐ I will give daily exercise and regularly bathe and groom.

I will be responsible for my dog's safety.

☐ I will properly control my dog by providing fencing where appropriate, by not letting my dog run loose, and by using a leash in public.

☐ I will ensure that my dog has some form of identification when appropriate (which may include collar tags, tattoos, or microchip identification).

☐ I will provide adequate supervision when my dog and children are together.

I will not allow my dog to infringe on the rights of others.

☐ I will not allow my dog to run loose in the neighborhood.

☐ I will not allow my dog to be a nuisance to others by barking while in the yard, in a hotel room, etc.

☐ I will pick up and properly dispose of my dog's waste in all public areas, such as on the grounds of hotels, on sidewalks, in parks, etc.

☐ I will pick up and properly dispose of my dog's waste in wilderness areas, on hiking trails, on campgrounds, and in off-leash parks.

I will be responsible for my dog's quality of life.

☐ I understand that basic training is beneficial to all dogs.

☐ I will give my dog attention and playtime.

☐ I understand that owning a dog is a commitment in time and caring.

The Dachshund in Miniature

Miniature Dachshunds began to be seen in Germany during the 19th century, although these "dwarf Dachshunds" looked nothing like the lovely dogs we see today. Crossbred with Dandie Dinmont Terriers, Miniature Pinschers, and Miniature Schnauzers, these early Minis were scruffy and inconsistent, most barely recognizable as Dachshunds. They were bred to rid the countryside of an exploding rabbit population, and their smaller frames were more effective against these quick, burrowing prey animals.

explain these unique personalities. The wirehaired Dachshund tends to be a bit more feisty and dominant, reflecting terrier crosses such as the Dandie Dinmont Terrier and the Miniature Schnauzer. Wires are often described as the clowns of the bunch and enjoy being the center of attention. The longhaired Dachshund has the sweetest and most biddable temperament, giving due credit to crosses with spaniels. Smooth Dachshunds are often said to be more determined and independent—willful, if you will—than their long- and wirehaired brethren, but these are pure Dachshund qualities no matter which coat type you choose.

How house-proud are you? Can you live with a little hair on your carpets? One variety of Dachshund does not shed, and it's not the smooth. The smooth loses those tiny little hairs every day, and the longhaired sheds even more. The wirehaired does not shed and is the best choice for an owner who's concerned about good housekeeping. Of the three varieties, however, the wirehaired does require the most grooming because the coat needs to be stripped (a grooming method done with a stripping knife or a well-trained thumb). Stripping is quite an art, and it takes a bit of know-how and practice to get your wirehaired Doxie to look his best. Many owners opt to hire a professional groomer to maintain the wire coat or, at the very least, to demonstrate the correct way to do it. Even if you're not showing your dog, stripping the wirehaired coat is the best way to retain the coat's natural, desirable texture.

CITY, COUNTRY, OR 'BURBS

While Dachshunds are social dogs that enjoy the company of humans and other dogs, they are also thoroughly self-sufficient. This special trait makes the breed far more adaptable than most, happy to live in any environment or climate. Given the choice, most dogs would choose to live in the open-air space of the country with a nice 60-degree Fahrenheit climate. California wine country would suffice for most Dachshunds! However, Dachshunds are equally at home in big cities, suburbs, campgrounds, or beachfront property. As long as the dog can get in his daily exercise and a little exploring, he will be happy and upbeat.

Whether you live in the city or the country, the Dachshund doesn't require a particularly large home. Even if you live in a small studio apartment, you will be glad to know that you can still thoroughly enjoy a happy life with a Dachshund, provided you don't neglect regular outdoor walks.

Dachshunds adjust to life in the big city in a New York minute, and they happily contribute to the reputation of the Big Apple as the "city that never sleeps." Keep in mind that your Dachshund is a vocal dog. Your next-door neighbors may not appreciate your hound dog's baying and crooning. Remember also that fifth-floor walkups are a bad idea for this long-backed dog—the Dachshund is an elevator dog. Miniatures are fairly easy to carry, if necessary, but Standards are less portable for average people. When you're shopping for an apartment that's above the third floor, make sure there's an elevator.

The Dachshund is also a clever escape artist, so suburbanites should take the time to walk around their yard and check that the fence is sturdy and securely anchored into the

The elegant longhair is perhaps the easiest of the Dachshund bunch to train.

Get to Know the AKC

AMERICAN KENNEL CLUB™

The country's leading canine organization, the American Kennel Club is a not-for-profit organization dedicated to the betterment and promotion of purebred dogs as family companions. The AKC is the largest and most prestigious dog registry in the United States. It was founded in 1884 with the mission of "upholding its registry and promoting the sport of pure-bred dogs and breeding for type and function." Supporting everything from health and wellness to breed standards to fun activities for the whole family, the AKC thrives on the participation of dog lovers like you.

Help continue the legacy by registering your pure-bred Dachshund with the AKC. It's as simple as filling out the Dog Registration Application you received when you bought your puppy and mailing it to the AKC in North Carolina, or register online at www.akc.org/dogreg.

The adaptable Dachshund will be happy to live anywhere with his favorite person.

ground. A puppy can easily squeeze through any small crevices that may exist. In Germany, Dachshunds are measured by the circumference of their chests, indicating how small of a hole they can fit through. Keep that in mind when your Dachshund begins burrowing his way under your chain-link fence! Survey your property periodically to make sure that your dog hasn't begun to dig his escape route. It's a good idea to install padlocks on your gates and, as an added precaution, put up "Close the Gate" signs. Your Dachshund will be off in a flash if someone is careless enough to leave your gate open.

EXERCISE NEEDS

Even though Dachshunds don't require endless hours of exercise, they do enjoy the opportunity to get outside and stretch their limbs—however short they are! If you can take your adult Doxie on two half-mile walks a day, it will keep him mentally and physically well balanced. Don't overdo it with seniors or puppies. You'll be doing your puppy no favors by exercising him for more than twenty minutes a day until he's one year of age. The puppy's muscles and bones are still developing, and too much exercise can cause unneeded stress on the dog. Adults can handle

significantly more exercise, and going an extra block or two does wonders to burn calories around the Dachshund's middle—and remember, he's all middle.

Dismantling boredom is another great advantage of that time spent around the neighborhood. A dog that's had a nice long walk is less likely to spend an hour barking at blue jays and wayward moths. It's not good to allow a dog as destructive—we mean, "creative"—as the Dachshund to become bored. You'll find that your dog is determined to make his own fun, and you won't approve of his methods. If you have a well-manicured lawn or landscaped garden surrounding your home, take heed. A Dachshund can redesign your backyard in less than fifteen minutes. He'll have the time of his life making tracks among your ferns and day lilies. Remember this mantra: exercise your Dachshund and save your marigolds!

Growing puppies need gentle exercise and time to rest as their bodies develop.

At a Glance ...

Although the shortest breed in the Hound Group, the Dachshund's personality is anything but small. The Dachshund's natural intelligence and trainability recommend him to dog lovers young and old who admire this wonderful breed for its countless positive attributes, including its bright personality and unshakable loyalty.

· ·

The Dachshund comes in two sizes, three coat varieties, and an assortment of colors and patterns. Despite their physical differences, all Dachshunds share the same outgoing traits and strong wills.

· ·

His legs may be short, but the busy, curious Dachshund still needs exercise. Keep your Dachshund physically and mentally stimulated with at least two walks a day and activities to keep him healthy and well behaved.

The Design of the Dachshund

What is a Dachshund? A little canine character with an extroverted personality and an ability to act the fool on occasion. This faithful, friendly breed should never be nervous or aggressive and is clever, lively, and courageous to the point of rashness. The highly versatile Dachshund is a passionate and persevering hunting dog that can work both above and below ground. He has an excellent nose and is a good tracker.

Some Dachshunds are more extroverted than others, but most become especially attached to one particular member of the family. Their choice is usually based on the person with whom they spend the most time. Dachshunds make great family dogs, especially the Standard variety. Standards are sturdier and more robust than Miniatures, and thus better able to withstand the lively play of children. Most Dachshunds love well-mannered children, but adult supervision and sensible guidance are always necessary.

PHYSICAL CONSTRUCTION

The Dachshund Club of America (DCA) standard divides Dachshunds into two sizes, Miniature and Standard. The Miniature weighs 11 pounds and under at twelve months of age and older. The Standard weighs between 16 and 32 pounds. Dachshunds that weigh between 11 and 16 pounds are called "Tweenies."

All Dachshunds are short-legged and have an elongated but compact build. Nonetheless, they are not restricted in movement, which must be free and flowing. The stride should be long, with drive from behind. Because of the Dachshund's original burrowing function, the front assembly is strong, deep, and cleanly muscled, with full ribs and a very prominent breastbone. The shoulders are well laid back, and the back is level. The tail is only slightly curved, with no kinks or twists.

The rump is strong, with clean muscles and joints forming right angles. When seen from behind, the Dachshund's legs should be set well apart, straight, and parallel. The front feet are full, broad, deep, and close-knit, making them suitable for digging. They may point straight ahead or can just slightly turn out. The hind feet are smaller, narrower, and forward-pointing. A Dachshund must stand "true," meaning equally on all parts of the feet.

The head of the Dachshund is long and tapers uniformly to the tip of the nose. The ridges over the eyes are prominent; the stop (the area between the eyes) is not. The muzzle is slightly arched. Complete dentition is important in the Dachshund. The teeth are powerful in a regular scissors bite, meaning that the outer sides of the lower incisors touch the inner sides of the upper incisors. The standard considers an even bite to be a minor fault, but any other bite that deviates from the correct scissors bite is a serious fault. The medium-sized, almond-shaped eyes of the Dachshund are energetic, giving a pleasant expression. In most colors, the eyes are dark, but they can be lighter in chocolates. Wall eyes (whitish irises; blue eyes) may be present in dappled dogs only. Dachshunds' ears are set high and not too far forward. They are broad, of moderate length, and well rounded, with the forward edge touching the cheek so that the ears frame the face.

A VERY COLORFUL BREED

The Dachshund is definitely a colorful breed, befitting the lively character of this remarkable dog that so easily captures people's hearts. All Dachshund coats have a base of either a solid color, such as red or cream (which may have shadings of interspersed dark hairs), or two colors, such as black, chocolate, blue (gray), and fawn (Isabella), always accompanied by rich tan or cream

The range of coat types, colors, and patterns produces many striking looks in the Dachshund.

markings. These markings are found over the eyes, on the sides of the jaw, on the inner edges of the ears, on the paws, on the front of the chest, around the anus, and on the underside of the tail. Red, cream, and black-and-tan Dachshunds should have black noses, black eye rims, black nails, and dark eyes. Chocolates, blues, and fawns have brown or self-colored noses, nails, and eye rims. They have lighter eyes than their red, cream, and black-and-tan cousins do, but the darker, the better. On all colors, a small amount of white on the chest is acceptable, but not desirable, according to the breed standard.

A PIECE OF HISTORY

At the beginning of World War I, Dachshunds were popular enough to be among the ten largest entries at the Westminster Kennel Club dog show. Soon, however, Americans disdained everything from Germany and viewed Dachshund owners as traitors. The breed suffered greatly until the end of the war, when new imports helped to rebuild bloodlines in the United States. Fortunately, World War II did not result in hostility toward the Dachshund, and the breed continued to thrive, ranking number six in AKC registrations for the decade of the 1940s.

STOP

WITHERS

BACK

MUZZLE

CHEST

BRISKET

ELBOW

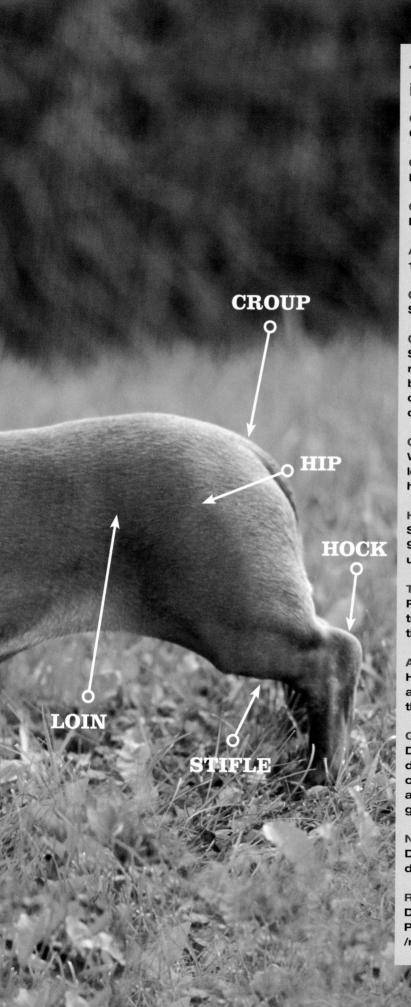

CROUP

HIP

HOCK

LOIN

STIFLE

The Dachshund in Brief

COUNTRY OF ORIGIN:
Germany

ORIGINAL USE:
Badger hunting

GROUP:
Hound

AVERAGE LIFE SPAN:
12 to 16 years

COAT:
Smooth, longhaired, or wirehaired.

COLORS:
Solid colors from cream to deep red; wild boar; bicolors including black, chocolate, and fawn with tan or cream markings. Patterns include dapple, piebald, brindle, and sable.

GROOMING:
Weekly brushing for smooth and longhaired coats; wirehairs require hand-stripping. Bathe monthly.

HEIGHT/WEIGHT:
Standard: 16 to 32 pounds and 8 to 9 inches; Miniature: 11 pounds and under and 5 to 6 inches.

TRAINABILITY:
Positive reinforcement and low-cal treats are training essentials with this breed.

ACTIVITY LEVEL:
High. Dachshunds are busy dogs and need to have activities to keep them from becoming bored.

GOOD WITH OTHER PETS:
Dachshunds are good with other dogs and can be trained to tolerate cats; they can't be trusted with small animals such as fancy rats, rabbits, guinea pigs, hamsters, and gerbils.

NATIONAL BREED CLUB:
Dachshund Club of America; www. dachshund-dca.org

RESCUE:
Dachshund Club of America Rescue Program; www.dachshund-dca.org /rescue.html

A BEVY OF PATTERNS

Any of the base colors can either stand alone or be accompanied by patterns that create different colorations. There are varying opinions as to whether wild boar should be considered a color or a pattern, but the breed standard describes it very well, stating that wild boar "...appears as banding of the individual hairs and imparts an overall grizzled effect which is most often seen on wirehaired Dachshunds, but may also appear on other coats. ...Variations include red boar and chocolate and tan boar."

Brindle is regularly seen in the Dachshund, producing varying amounts of black or dark striping over the entire body. In some dogs, the brindle may be visible only in the tan or cream points because dark stripes will not be evident on the black parts of the coat.

More rare is the sable pattern, which places a very distinctive, uniform dark overlay on red dogs, the overlay hairs having darker tips than the base color. This pattern typically displays a widow's peak on the head.

Dapple is a very interesting pattern in the Dachshund. The breed standard defines it as follows: "The dapple (merle) pattern is expressed as lighter-colored areas contrasting with the darker base color, which may be any acceptable color.

The wire coat should not conceal the Dachshund's unique outline.

Neither the light nor the dark color should predominate.... A large area of white on the chest of a dapple is permissible." At least one parent must be a dapple in order to produce this pattern in the offspring. The pattern can be difficult to identify in red dogs, where light patches might be hard to detect. Black-and-tan dapples are sometimes referred to as "silver dapples" because of the silvery color that the merle gene imparts to the black hairs it affects.

Double dapple is a term used for the pattern in which varying amounts of white occur on the body in addition to the base color and the dapple pattern. This pattern is produced only when two dapples are bred to each other. While double-dapple Dachshunds can be registered with the American Kennel Club, the pattern is not listed in the breed standard. The standard's purpose is to describe the ideal Dachshund, and serious health problems can accompany the double-dapple pattern, blindness and deafness being the most common.

Piebald is another pattern that can be registered with the AKC but is not described in the breed standard. Piebald Dachshunds have large areas of white hair appearing on any base color, but the pattern is most often seen on black-and-tan or red Dachshunds. The piebald pattern can be confusing because, for example, on a red piebald, it may appear that the red areas are patches when, in reality, the dog's base color is red and the white areas are the patches.

THREE COATS

The smooth Dachshund, the original and the most popular of the three coat types in the United States, has dense, short, smooth hair, with coarser hair on the underside of the tail. On smooths, the skin is "elastic and pliable" (per the breed standard) yet close fitting with little or no wrinkle.

Likely developed from crosses with spaniels, the longhaired Dachshund is the most glamorous of the three varieties, with a shiny coat comparable to that of the Irish Setter. The breed standard describes the longhaired coat: "The sleek, glistening, often slightly wavy hair is longer under the neck and on the forechest, the underside of the body, the ears, and behind the legs." The soft hair is straight or only slightly wavy, longest under the neck, underparts, behind the legs, and on the tail, where it forms a flag. The outside of the ears is well feathered, but there shouldn't be excess hair on the feet. The coat should never be so profuse that it masks the breed type, and the standard discourages curly coats or coats that are parted along the back.

The wirehaired Dachshund, perhaps the most extroverted of the three varieties, is covered with a short, straight, harsh coat, except on the jaw, eyebrows, chin, and ears. The whole body is covered with a dense undercoat. The bushy eyebrows and beard give the dog a smart, wise appearance, with a glint of mischief in his

Longhaired History

Early German woodcuts are evidence that longhaired Dachshunds have long existed in the breed, even though they have never been as popular as their smooth cousins. Some experts believe that the longhaired variety was the result of a spaniel (possibly a German land-and-water spaniel such as the Kleiner Münsterländer) and smooth Dachshund cross. Others believe that breeders who were enamored of the longer-coated puppies found in smooth litters embarked on a selective breeding program to produce the new coat type. The variety's docile, sweet temperament perhaps lends weight to the spaniel theory, but, of course, every dog is an individual.

eyes. The ears are almost smooth, and the legs and feet have a neat, harsh coat. The wire coat should never be curly or wavy. The standard says that the wirehair should resemble the smooth when viewed from a distance, indicating that the dog's coat should not be exaggerated or hide the natural outline of the dog. The wirehaired variety comes in all of the accepted Dachshund colors, but red, wild boar, and black and tan are the most popular colors for this variety in America.

CALLING ALL HOUNDS

The Hound Group, as designated by the American Kennel Club, consists of twenty-seven breeds, essentially categorized as scenthounds and sighthounds. The designation refers to the breed's style of hunting—whether it relies primarily upon its keen nose or its superior eyes. The badger-hunting Dachshund belongs to the nose side of the family, along with the Beagle, the English and American Foxhounds, the Harrier, the Basset Hound, and the Petit Basset Griffon Vendéen, all of which were bred to hunt fox and rabbit. The Otterhound was named for its quarry—otter—just as the Dachshund was named for badgers. There are six raccoon-hunting hounds in the Group, namely the Black and Tan Coonhound, the Bluetick Coonhound, the Treeing Walker Coonhound, the Redbone Coonhound, the American English Coonhound, and the Plott. The Plott was also bred to pursue large game, as was the Rhodesian Ridgeback, Norwegian Elkhound, and the nose of all noses, the Bloodhound.

Scenthounds share many similar characteristics in terms of behavior and conformation. They are determined and enduring when in pursuit of their quarry, blessed with large, musical voices and an innate ability to track down a lost person or wounded animal. The Dachshund is indeed the shortest of the scenthounds, and the Bloodhound, standing at 27 inches, is one of the tallest. All of these dogs are built for "moving out"—running at great speeds and/or distances—on their strong-boned legs and well-arched toes. Although most scenthounds possess smooth hair, a few—such as the Petit Basset Griffon Vendéen and the Otterhound—have wire coats. Of course, the Dachshund comes in smooth, wirehaired, and longhaired varieties.

HOUND OR TERRIER?

The European classification of the Dachshund as its own Group may be the perfect nonanswer for the question, "Is the Dachshund a hound or a terrier?" Terriers, by definition, are earthdogs, and the Dachshund was built for digging as much as any "going-to-ground" terrier. The breed was designed to enter the burrow of a badger or the hole of a rabbit, throwing dirt and gravel out of its way while pressing toward its quarry. While "cat feet" are called for in almost all of the scenthound and terrier breeds, scenthounds are not specifically built for digging. Several authoritative nineteenth-century volumes on dogs did in fact classify the Dachshund as a terrier.

Dachshunds have the scenting-hound apparatus—the elongated muzzle; long, abundant ears; and the large, open nose—required to trail, and they have the "strong, deep, long, and cleanly muscled" front needed for "effective underground work," as the DCA standard describes. The General Appearance

A smooth coat glistens in rich red.

Meet the Dachshund

AMERICAN
KENNEL CLUB™

A great place to see Dachshunds and more than 200 other dog and cat breeds is at AKC Meet the Breeds®, hosted by the American Kennel Club and presented by Pet Partners, Inc. Not only can you see dogs, cats, puppies, and kittens of all sizes, you can also talk to experts in each of the breeds. Meet the Breeds features demonstration rings to watch events with law enforcement K9s, grooming, agility, and obedience. You also can browse the more than 100 vendor booths for every imaginable product for you and your pet.

It's great fun for the whole family. Meet the Breeds takes place in the fall in New York City. For more information, check out www.meetthebreeds.com.

Excerpts from the Breed Standard

AMERICAN
KENNEL CLUB™

General Appearance

Low to ground, long in body and short of leg, with robust muscular development; the skin is elastic and pliable without excessive wrinkling. Appearing neither crippled, awkward, nor cramped in his capacity for movement, the Dachshund is well-balanced with bold and confident head carriage and intelligent, alert facial expression. NOTE: Inasmuch as the Dachshund is a hunting dog, scars from honorable wounds shall not be considered a fault.

Size, Proportion, Substance

Bred and shown in two sizes, standard and miniature; miniatures are not a separate classification but compete in a class division for "11 pounds and under at 12 months of age and older." Weight of the standard size is usually between 16 and 32 pounds.

Head

Viewed from above or from the side, the head tapers uniformly to the tip of the nose. The eyes are of medium size, almond-shaped and dark-rimmed, with an energetic, pleasant expression; not piercing; very dark in color. The ears are set near the top of the head, not too far forward, of moderate length, rounded, not narrow, pointed, or folded. The skull is slightly arched, neither too broad nor too narrow, and slopes gradually with little perceptible stop into the finely-formed, slightly arched muzzle, giving a Roman appearance. Nostrils well open. Jaws ... with strongly developed bones and teeth. *Teeth*—Powerful canine teeth; teeth fit closely together in a scissors bite.

Neck

Long, muscular, clean-cut, without dewlap, slightly arched in the nape, flowing gracefully into the shoulders without creating the impression of a right angle.

Trunk

The trunk is long and fully muscled. When viewed in profile, the back lies in the straightest possible line between the withers and the short, very slightly arched loin. *Abdomen*—Slightly drawn up.

Forequarters

Chest—The breast-bone is strongly prominent in front so that on either side a depression or dimple appears. The keel ... extends well beyond the front legs. *Shoulder blades*—Long, broad, well-laid back ... *Upper Arm* ... strong of bone and hard of muscle, lying close to the ribs, with elbows close to the body, yet capable of free movement. *Forearm*—Short; supplied with hard yet pliable muscles on the front and outside ... The inclined shoulder blades, upper arms and curved forearms form parentheses that enclose the ribcage, creating the correct "wraparound front." *Feet*—Front paws are full, tight, compact, with well-arched toes and tough, thick pads. They may be equally inclined a trifle outward.

Hindquarters

Strong and cleanly muscled ... the thighs are strong and powerful. The legs turn neither in nor out. *Rear pasterns*—Short and strong, perpendicular to the second thigh bone. When viewed from behind, they are upright and parallel. *Feet*— Smaller than the front paws with four compactly closed and arched toes with tough, thick pads. *Croup*—Long, rounded and full, sinking slightly toward the tail. *Tail*—Set in continuation of the spine.

Gait

Fluid and smooth. Forelegs reach well forward, without much lift, in unison with the driving action of hind legs. Hind legs drive on a line with the forelegs, with hock joints and rear pasterns (metatarsus) turning neither in nor out.

—from the Dachshund Club of America Breed Standard

paragraph of the standard begins the discussion: "His hunting spirit, good nose, loud tongue and distinctive build make him well-suited for below-ground work and for beating the bush. His keen nose gives him an advantage over most other breeds for trailing."

At field trials, Dachshunds always hunt rabbit or hare, and they are expected to enter a rabbit lodge without hesitation. Additionally, the dogs are judged on nose, perseverance, keenness, and courage to endure any cover no matter how punishing.

A longhaired puppy's elegant furnishings take time to develop.

At a Glance ...

The Dachshund's unique and recognizable physique was bred for a specific purpose. A hound at heart, the Dachshund also possesses a broad chest; short, powerful legs; and a long body that were designed to "go to ground" after prey such as badgers, rabbits, and foxes.

· ·

In addition to the breed's two sizes and three coat varieties, Dachshunds are seen in a multitude of colors and patterns. Each Dachshund is one of a kind in the combination of its stature, coat type, and color.

· ·

The Dachshund is the smallest of the scenthounds in the AKC Hound Group. Although the breed is often labeled as a terrier due to its roots as an earthdog, Dachshunds are blessed with keen scenting capabilities and physical traits that help him track prey by scent: an elongated muzzle; long, drooping ears; and a wide, open nose.

Let's Get a Doxie!

Which Dachshund size do you prefer—Standard or Miniature? Most Doxie lovers can answer that question automatically, but deciding on which of the three coat types they want may take more thought. The smooth coat requires the least maintenance, though shedding is still an issue. The long coat needs to be brushed regularly to avoid tangling, and the wire coat, although it doesn't shed, needs

WHY CHOOSE A BREEDER?

Once you know which size and coat type you prefer, you can narrow down the list of Dachshund breeders to those who specialize in that variety. Never rush into buying a puppy. If you have to wait awhile to get the puppy you want, then so be it. The wait will be well worth it.

Prospective puppy buyers should be aware that there are different kinds of breeders, some with the breed's best interest at heart, others with financial gain in mind. It's best to find a breeder with dogs you admire and at least ten years of experience in the breed. With a breed as structurally unique as the Dachshund,

Get Your Registration and Pedigree

AMERICAN KENNEL CLUB™

A responsible breeder will be able to provide your family with an American Kennel Club registration form and pedigree.

AKC REGISTRATION: When you buy a Dachshund from a breeder, ask the breeder for an American Kennel Club Dog Registration Application form. The breeder will fill out most of the application for you. When you fill out your portion of the document and mail it to the AKC, you will receive a Registration Certificate, proving that your dog is officially part of the AKC. Besides recording your name and your dog's name in the AKC database, registration helps fund the AKC's good works, such as canine health research, search-and-rescue teams, educating the public about responsible dog care, and much more.

CERTIFIED PEDIGREE: A pedigree is an AKC certificate that proves your dog is a purebred. It shows your puppy's family tree, listing the names of his parents and grandparents. If your dog is registered with the AKC, the organization will have a copy of your dog's pedigree on file, which you can order from its website (www.akc.org). Look for any titles that your Dachshund's ancestors have won, including Champion (conformation), Companion Dog (obedience), and so forth. A pedigree doesn't guarantee the health or personality of a dog, but it's a starting point for picking out a good Dachshund puppy.

A good breeder ensures that the pups have adequate time with their mother for weaning and early socialization.

Did You Know?

The American Kennel Club sponsors a program for responsible and trusted breeders called the AKC Breeder of Merit program. Breeders who register their litters with the AKC, are members of AKC-affiliated clubs, and have at least five years of involvement with AKC events are eligible to apply as AKC Breeders of Merit. Breeders must have earned at least four conformation, performance, or companion titles with dogs that they have bred or co-bred. If your breeder is an AKC Breeder of Merit participant, you can rest assured that he or she is a good choice for your future Dachshund puppy.

you are well advised to find a breeder who has the requisite know-how to breed sound dogs and raise healthy litters.

There are many good breeders around, and, if you look carefully, you will find just such a person. The AKC and the Dachshund Club of America are trusted sources from which to find referrals, and both have great websites with breeder pages organized by state. The Dachshund Club of America recommends that all puppy buyers purchase their puppies from responsible breeders who breed Dachshunds for exhibition or performance competition. Pet-puppy buyers are often impulsive and don't want to wait for a good puppy from a reputable breeder. Because this puppy will likely be spending well more than a decade with you, there's no reason to rush into choosing the wrong puppy. Buying a puppy from a show breeder increases your chances of finding a typical, sound, and healthy puppy, a Dachshund that will grow up to look like a Dachshund and will have all of the qualities that attracted you to the breed in the first place.

Because responsible breeders breed dogs to conform to the breed standard, the offspring of champion dogs will most likely look like the dog you want. Responsible breeders pride themselves on screening their stock for potential hereditary and congenital disorders, improving the odds that puppies will be born healthy and sound. In addition to appearance and soundness, show breeders concern themselves with the good temperaments of their progeny. No matter how handsome or healthy a dog is, if he's not friendly and trustworthy, he has no value as a companion. Breeders who breed good-natured, confident dogs and invest time in socialization produce puppies that are neither shy nor aggressive.

Purebred-dog aficionados take pride in the predictability of each breed. At just a few weeks of age, a breeder can predict how a Collie, Bulldog, or Dachshund puppy will look and behave when he grows up. With prior knowledge of the generations of dogs in his or her own line, a good breeder can even more accurately predict a dog's future structure and personality. For example, a breeder knows precisely when a dog's adult coat and color will develop and when his chest will drop. When an experienced breeder looks at one of his or her puppies and says, "This one is going to grow into a handsome, wild boar boy," you can trust that the statement is true! Further, responsible breeders will sell you a puppy at a fair price, often matching the pet-puppy prices of less experienced breeders.

FINDING THE RIGHT BREEDER

Begin your breeder search on the AKC's website (www.akc.org) to find a breeder. Your options will be greater depending on how far you're willing to drive. The breeders listed on the AKC website are likely members of AKC-licensed or member clubs and are possibly AKC Breeder of Merit participants. The AKC does not endorse the breeders who advertise litters on its website, but it's an excellent starting point. You should also visit the Dachshund Club of America's website (www.dachshund-dca.org), where you can find a roster of member breeders who may have puppies available.

Find a breeder with a reputation in your chosen variety of Dachshund.

Visiting an AKC dog show is another way to make contact with breeders. The AKC website includes an event calendar that lists dog shows around the country. Dog shows take place on most weekends of the year as well as on many weekdays. Most responsible breeders participate in dog shows or other AKC events because they regard the ring as the testing grounds of their breeding programs. A championship title essentially tells the public that at least three highly qualified show judges have assessed the dog and evaluated it superior to all of the other Dachshunds in the show—and that the dog is worthy of being bred.

While you're at the dog show, purchase a catalog, which lists all of the dogs competing in each class for that day. As you're watching each Dachshund being judged, you can identify the owner, breeder, and handler of the dog by matching the number on the handler's armband with the number listed in the catalog. (If the letter "S," "L," or "W" follows a Dachshund's name, it indicates his coat type, and "M" or "S" refers to Miniature or Standard.) The catalog also provides contact information for the owners. Get a feeling

The Dachshund's long, low profile is evident from birth.

How to Recognize a Good Breeder

• The breeder welcomes questions about the breed and his or her breeding program.

• He or she is clearly devoted to the breed and has been involved with the breed for ten years or more.

• He or she shows his or her own dogs or places them with handlers to exhibit at dog shows.

• The breeder belongs to the Dachshund Club of America and is a member in good standing.

• He or she screens the breeding stock for health concerns.

• The breeder asks you sensible questions about your home life, experience with owning a dog, why you're interested in the Dachshund, and what your intentions are for the puppy.

• The breeder registers her dogs with the American Kennel Club and is an AKC Breeder of Merit participant.

for how the ring procedure works, and don't approach the handlers until they've finished in the ring. They will be happy to speak with you after the judging is complete, but it's important to let them concentrate while they are competing.

You will meet many experienced owners and breeders at shows, have the chance to meet their dogs, and make the acquaintance of people just like you who live to "talk Dachshund." After a few brief conversations with true Doxie lovers, you'll know whether or not you've got Dachshunds in your blood, too. Newcomers to the breed are served best to listen, listen, listen, because Dachshund people have valuable information to share. Dachshund people are as unique as their breed, and are just as determined and devoted as their chosen dogs.

VISITING THE BREEDER

Once you contact a breeder, you still need to be sure that his or her standards of care are what you expect. Follow up with a visit to the breeder's home or kennel. The breeder you select is most likely someone who breeds from his or her home, in which case the puppies will have been brought up in the house and will be familiar with the daily activities and noises of a home. That's not to say that all good breeders only raise their dogs in their homes. Some very reputable breeders run larger establishments in which litters are whelped and raised in kennels or other auxiliary buildings. Responsible breeders will still socialize these puppies and expose them to the sounds and sights of the breeders' homes and families.

However large or small the breeding establishment, it is important that the conditions in which the puppies are raised are suitable. The areas should be clean, and the puppies should be outgoing and friendly. The puppies should appear happy, squeaky-clean, and ready for action. They should be approachable and confident, with courage "to the point of rashness."

The breeder should be happy to present the dam (mother) of the litter to you. Responsible breeders take great pride in their dams, though you should be aware that she may not look as glamorous and fresh as she might in the show ring. Nursing, training, and chasing a litter of rowdy Doxie babies for four or five weeks can take the *oomph* out of the best of Dachshund mothers. Even so, you should consider her temperament, how she interacts with her offspring, and how friendly she is toward you. Take note also of the breeder's rapport with the dam: it's a great indicator of the kind of dog lover the breeder is. If the dam is not available for you to see, this might be a sign that the puppies were not born on the premises, but were brought in from elsewhere to be sold. You should consider continuing your puppy search elsewhere.

As for the sire (father) of the litter, it is likely that he will not be available, for he may well be owned by someone else. An experienced breeder may have traveled a great distance to use the sire's stud services. Nonetheless, dedicated breeders will be able to show you at least the sire's pedigree and a picture of him, as well as tell you about him and his background.

A well-chosen breeder will give new puppy owners much useful guidance, including advice about feeding, training, vet visits, and so forth. Some breeders give a small quantity of puppy food to new owners to help the puppies adjust

The quality of a breeder's adult dogs tells volumes about the quality of the puppies.

Why Should You Register with the American Kennel Club?

Registering your puppy with the American Kennel Club helps the AKC do many good things for dogs everywhere, such as promote responsible breeding and support the care and health of dogs throughout the country. As a result of your registration, the AKC is able to inspect kennels across the country, educate dog owners about the importance of training through the Canine Good Citizen® Program, support search-and-rescue canines via the AKC Companion Animal Recovery Canine Support and Relief Fund, teach the public about the importance of responsible dog ownership through publications and the annual AKC Responsible Dog Ownership Days, and much more. Not only is the AKC a respected organization dedicated to the purebred dog, but it is also devoted to the well-being of all dogs everywhere. For more information, visit www.akc.org.

Dachshund Rescue

Anyone can buy a Dachshund, though not everyone is worthy of owning a member of this noble clan. Too often, people buy dogs without investing time in researching the breed or the source. Some people simply are unable to keep their Dachshunds due to changes in living or work situations, finances, or other personal problems. Hundreds of unwanted Dachshunds in need of homes are available around the country, and many of these dogs can make ideal companions. If you're interested in adopting an adult rescue dog, contact the Dachshund Club of America (DCA). The DCA has a national rescue network, and you can contact representatives from your state (or a nearby state) by visiting the Dachshund Club of America Rescue Program online at www.dachshund-dca.org/rescue.html.

to their new homes. In any event, the breeder should always provide written details of exactly what type and quantity of food the puppy has been fed, and how often. You will, of course, be able to change this as time goes on, but don't change the puppy's food right away. You can do so gradually if necessary.

A breeder will also tell you what vaccinations the puppy has received and give you all details about the puppy's preventive wormings. Many breeders will also provide some type of health guarantee, which will allow you to return the puppy for any reason. A responsible breeder cares deeply about the well-being of his or her puppies. In addition to health documents, the breeder should give you a copy of the pedigree, AKC registration papers, sales contract, and guarantee.

CHOOSING A PUPPY

Once you have decided on a breeder, visit the litter when the puppies are around five or six weeks of age. No matter how ready you think you are, you must wait a few more weeks before your puppy is ready to come home with you. Responsible breeders will not release puppies until they are at least eight to twelve weeks of age, fully weaned from their dams and ready for the real world.

A healthy puppy should be clean, with no sign of discharge from the eyes or nose, and have a distinctive clean-puppy smell. His rear end should be spotless, with no sign of loose droppings. Puppy nails can be sharp, but the breeder should keep them well trimmed.

The puppy's coat should be shiny and vibrant, with no sign of parasites. It's not always easy to see fleas and lice, but infested puppies will scratch incessantly or possibly have rashes on their bellies. Scratching, though, does not always indicate a skin condition, for it can also be associated with teething. In this case, the puppy will only scratch around his head area, and this will stop after the teething period, around seven to eight months old. Scratching might also be a symptom of an ear infection, so a quick look inside the pup's ears will ensure that there is no odor or buildup of wax. Of course, a good breeder will have checked that all of the puppies are in good health.

Most puppies are outgoing and full of fun, so do not take pity on the overly shy one that hides away in a corner. Your puppy should clearly enjoy your company when you visit. When you go to select your puppy, take the members of your immediate family with you. It is essential that everyone in the household agrees with the important decision you are about to make. If you decide to take your children along to visit the litter, you must take care that they are very gentle and do not frighten the puppies with loud noises or quick, unexpected actions. Don't be swayed by your children's enthusiasm for the puppies—they likely haven't researched the breed or read this chapter!

If the test exists, responsible breeders will screen their dogs for health issues before breeding. Find out what health clearances are recommended, as Dachshunds are at risk for certain hereditary conditions that concern breeders. These include diabetes, epilepsy, intervertebral disk disease (IVDD), cancer, autoimmune thyroid disease and hypothyroidism, and eye disorders. A responsible breeder will have clearances from the Orthopedic Foundation for Animals (OFA) and the Canine Eye Registration Foundation (CERF) for both the sire and dam of the litter. You should ask to see written proof of the results.

By now, you should realize that you must research the breed long before a new puppy enters your lives. The national parent club, the Dachshund Club of America, as well as regional breed clubs are important sources of help and information. Take advantage of these organizations and their websites.

It is a good idea to become a member of a regional Dachshund club as well as the national parent club. You will become acquainted with other Dachshund lovers and receive notification of various breed events near you, such as dog shows, earthdog trials, and field trials that you may like to attend.

At a Glance ...

Don't be surprised if your breeder asks more questions than you do! Responsible breeders care about the well-being of their puppies. Be prepared for the breeder to interview you about your home, lifestyle, and plans for your puppy's future.

. . . .

Choose a healthy Dachshund puppy—one with bright eyes, a clean body, and an outgoing personality. Don't be tempted to buy a shy, unhealthy puppy with a vow to give him a good home. The choice will only end in excessive veterinary bills and heartache.

. . . .

Don't leave the breeder's home without a puppy sales contract, the pedigree and AKC registration papers, and the appropriate health certificates. A responsible breeder will provide you with all of these items without hesitation, and he or she will stand by the good health and breeding of your new Dachshund puppy.

A Hound in Your Home

Whether you're ten years old or ten times ten, you can relive the excitement of Christmas morning! Awaiting the arrival of a new puppy recaptures that same sort of excitement. In this case, though, you must be completely prepared so that everything is ready and waiting for your new family member.

Where will the new puppy sleep? Where will you place his crate and bed? What rooms will the puppy have access to? Do you have a safe, reliable

way to confine the puppy to his designated area? Have you checked the yard to make sure that there are no holes in your fencing or other hidden escape routes? Have you made the requisite trip to the pet-supply store to purchase the many items that your puppy is likely to need during his first week with you?

Take advantage of your breeder's experience and ask him or her for a list of things that he or she recommends for your new puppy. The breeder's advice on the best kind of leash and collar, food dishes, food, shampoo, and other supplies for your Dachshund is invaluable to you and will take away some of the guess-work and experimentation that goes into first-time puppy ownership. Breeders want to ensure that their puppies have the best of everything, so discuss exactly what your puppy will need to make his life healthy, safe, and enjoyable.

WHERE TO START?

Unless you live in a very remote area, there's probably a good pet-supply store within driving distance of your home. A pet superstore or a well-stocked, privately owned pet shop will offer many options for everything that you need.

Plan ahead and be sure that your shopping list is complete before you walk into the pet store. The major pet-supply chains often have helpful sales assistants who know the merchandise well. If your local pet store is an independent shop owned by real dog people, it will have a wide range of dog supplies, from the basics to fun specialty items. With any luck, you'll be able to get sensible guidance at either type of outlet. Visiting a large all-breed dog show is another dog-supply bonanza, as shows often have dozens of trade stands that offer the latest and

It's an exciting time when you're awaiting the arrival of your new family member.

greatest of everything. At these trade stands, you will definitely find knowledgeable dog folk who will give you advice on what's best for your Dachshund.

THE ESSENTIALS

Depending on which variety of Dachshund you've chosen, there are certain specific grooming items that you will need. Ask your breeder which types of brushes and combs he or she recommends for your dog's coat type. In addition to these items, you'll also need a doggy toothbrush and toothpaste, a nail clipper, and some doggy shampoo for your Dachshund's basic grooming.

Having plenty of safe dog toys on hand will prevent your puppy from choosing his own playthings.

Select a dog crate that is sensibly sized for a full-grown Dachshund. There's no sense purchasing a second crate when the dog grows longer! If you've never used a crate for your dog, welcome to the new century! While dog crates haven't had the impact on society that, say, computers or cell phones have had, they're definitely just as important. The crate is the best possible tool for house-training your Dachshund, and it offers your pup a safe, cozy place to call his own for naps, bedtime, and just to relax.

TIME TO SHOP!

Before the puppy comes home, be sure you've collected everything he will need. You will be very busy once the new pup arrives, so it's wise to purchase all of your puppy items as soon as you've given the breeder a deposit.

A PIECE OF HISTORY

Recognized by the American Kennel Club in 1885, the Dachshund didn't make its first appearance on the AKC's top ten list until the 1940s. The breed's popularity continued to climb through the next two decades, ranking number five in the 1950s and number four in the 1960s. The breed has remained in the top ten ever since. It reached the number-three position seven times: 1957 (behind the Beagle and the Chihuahua), 1961 (behind the Poodle and the Beagle); 1968, 1969, and 1970 (behind the Poodle and the German Shepherd Dog); and 1998 and 1999 (behind the Labrador and the Poodle). In 2011, the Dachshund was number nine in AKC registrations, and in 2012, the breed was number ten.

Choose toys that will keep your puppy's interest and withstand the wear and tear of chewing.

Bowls: You'll find plastic, pottery, and stainless steel among the choices. The least aesthetic choice, in this case, will be your best bet: stainless steel. It can't be destroyed by puppy teeth, it can be sanitized easily, and it's virtually indestructible. Purchase bowls for indoors—one for food and one for water—and an extra bowl for water outside. They're affordable, and you likely won't have to replace them. Once your Dachshund is older and less likely to chew, you may want to explore some

Consider the Microchip

In addition to using a dog collar and ID tag, think about having your veterinarian insert a microchip in your dog to help find him if he ever gets lost. When scanned, the microchip will show your dog's unique microchip number so that your Dachshund can be returned to you as soon as possible. Go to www.akccar.org to learn more about the nonprofit American Kennel Club Companion Animal Recovery (AKC CAR) pet recovery system.

Since 1995, the AKC CAR service has been selected by millions of dog owners who are grateful for the peace of mind and service that AKC CAR offers.

As a smart owner, always keep in mind that your Dachshund is differently shaped than most other dogs. When holding your Dachshund, keep his back horizontal, with his hind quarters under your arm and your hands under his chest. This "cradling the football" position is the best for his back. If your Dachshund is going to spend time on the couch or bed with you, set up a ramp for him to climb. Introduce the puppy to the ramp, and he'll think this is the normal way to get down from furniture. Limiting his jumping avoids undue stress on your Doxie's fragile back.

more attractive options, coordinating with your kitchen's colors or style. Beware of plastic bowls, as bacteria can collect in the grooves of the plastic and cause an allergic reaction in some dogs. Purchase a mat for underneath the bowls to protect your floors from spills and crumbs.

Brushes and combs: For the smooth coat, you'll need a hound glove and a natural bristle brush; for the long coat, a natural bristle brush or pin brush and a medium-toothed metal comb; and for the wire coat, a slicker brush, a medium-toothed metal comb, and stripping knife. A flea comb, which is a fine-toothed metal comb, is handy for all three varieties. When shopping for these items, purchase the best quality you can. Cheaper tools fall apart, and you'll end up purchasing the more expensive ones later.

Crate: Don't hesitate to purchase a crate for your Dachshund. Take it with you to pick the puppy up from the breeder's home. The crate is the perfect tool for house-training your Dachshund, giving him his own sleeping quarters, and trans-

Many household items are surprisingly dangerous for your dog. As you puppy-proof your home, keep in mind all of those hidden places where you may keep cleaning supplies, car supplies, and backyard fertilizer and tools. Here are a few of the most common poisons found around the house and in the garage:

- Acetaminophen
- Antifreeze
- Bleach
- Boric acid
- Car fluids
- Cleaning fluids
- Deodorizers
- Detergents
- Disinfectants
- Drain cleaners
- Furniture polish
- Gasoline
- Herbicides
- Insecticides
- Kerosene
- Matches
- Mothballs
- Nail polish and remover
- Paint
- Prescription medication
- Rat poison
- Rubbing alcohol
- Snail or slug bait
- Turpentine

porting him in the car. Show folk were the first ones to promote crates for training, and today most trainers and breeders recommend crates for everyday canine life, whether the dog is a show dog, a home companion, or both. There are a few standard options: the fiberglass crate, the type required for airline travel; the wire crate, sturdy, collapsible, and allowing the best ventilation; and the fabric crate, the lightest and most portable, providing the least protection.

Crate pad: Pet stores sell comfortable pads that fit the bottom of a standard crate. A machine-washable pad will make the crate more cozy and soft for your young puppy. You can also just use towels in the crate to provide the same effect. Most dog folk have a stack of "dog towels" in their laundry room; if you don't, go buy yourself some nice new towels and hand your old ones down to your Doxie!

Bed: Choose a simple, medium-sized, circular or rectangular bed for your puppy. The puppy will welcome a nice soft bed to take a midday snooze on or to retreat to with a favorite toy. Choose a bed that can be laundered easily, such as one with a removable cover that can be unzipped. Once your Dachshund is older, you may want to purchase a more elaborate bed, but start with something affordable and washable. Dogs appreciate a clean bed, so wash the bed every couple of weeks, more often if the pup's had an accident. It's best to place the bed in a central location in the house, but not in a hallway or other high-traffic area, and always in a draft-free location. Avoid wicker beds or any bed that is temptingly chewable, as sharp pieces of wicker can scratch the puppy or, if swallowed, cause choking or internal injury. Keep all of your dog's bedding clean and dry.

Toys: Pups are like children—they live to play. Some Dachshunds never grow out of their toy-loving phase. Choose a few different kinds of toys to give your dog some variety, but don't max out your credit card buying one of each toy in your local pet-supply store. Too much selection can lead to a puppy feeling overwhelmed and frustrated. You can't go wrong with a sturdy squeaky toy, a bouncing ball, a rope toy, and a nylon or hard plastic bone. Dogs love rawhides, but most dogs devour them as if they're petrified food. Rawhide is not good for dogs' digestive systems, and large pieces can often get lodged in their throats. The safety of your dog should be your first consideration when selecting toys. Never buy cheap toys or those with removable parts that your Dachshund could easily swallow.

Gates and pens: Baby gates or puppy gates—depending on whether you buy them in a pet store or a people store—are great solutions to confining the puppy to a specific area of your home. If gates won't work in your home because you have an open floor plan with no doorways, then an exercise pen ("X-pen") may be your answer.

PUPPY-PROOFING

Once the puppy becomes comfortable in his surroundings—usually within a day or two, or perhaps an hour or two in the Dachshund's case—he will be ready to explore everywhere you permit him. All puppies are curious, and the slinky, slippery Dachshund will zip around your house and bury his nose and teeth into everything that he encounters. In order to keep your little Dachshund safe and to protect your home and belongings, you're wise to get on all fours and inspect the house from a dog's perspective before the puppy gets home.

Everyday items that you wouldn't think twice about become real concerns. Electrical cords, cable wires, wastebaskets, bathroom cabinets, toilet-bowl brushes, mops and buckets—the list goes on and on. Use common sense and err on the side of caution. Remove all household cleaners as well as items stored in your garage or shed, such as paint cans, antifreeze, fertilizers, windshield-wiper fluid, turpentine, and so forth, from your puppy's reach. These items will get your puppy sick, while others will kill him. At the very least, they will create a mess. Your laundry room is not puppy-friendly either—be sure that detergents, bleach, and dryer sheets are locked away from the puppy.

Get in the habit of picking up shoes, socks, stockings, and other items that your puppy can chew and possibly swallow. Many veterinarians tell horror stories about socks they've removed from dogs' intestines, not to mention thumb tacks, paper clips, and bobby pins.

A Dachshund's nose can lead him to "fun stuff" that you didn't even know about, so a thorough household cleaning is in order prior to the puppy's arrival. Sweep behind cabinets, shelves, couches, and other furniture so that your puppy doesn't find the bagel, sponge, or remote control you lost in the late 1990s. Look around the house for dangling fabric that the puppy can grab and pull, including drapes, tassels, tablecloths, and runners on tables. You don't want your Dachshund to destroy your possessions or to cause breakable items to land on the floor

Prepare your home for your Dachshund's safety both indoors and out.

or, worse, on his head. Remove candy dishes from coffee tables and put your bottom-shelf books in a box until the puppy's chewing phase is over.

Take care to remove houseplants from your puppy's reach because Dachshunds are instinctively attracted to dirt and greenery! Many common varieties of houseplants are poisonous to dogs, so you're wise to keep all plants away from your Doxie's paws, nose, and mouth. You have nothing to gain by your

Seasonal Safety Tips

SPRING	SUMMER	AUTUMN	WINTER
Be careful about which flowers you choose to plant in your yard; many are toxic to dogs.	Fresh, cool water should always be available whenever your dog is spending time outdoors.	Keep dogs off of grass that's been treated for the upcoming season.	Don't overdo outside time on very cold days; frostbite can happen faster than you think.
Outdoor plant fertilizers can kill dogs. Keep your digging Doxie away from your flower beds.	Dogs overheat quickly: shade in the backyard is essential.	Small dogs can get buried in piles of fallen leaves, and they dislike leaf blowers.	Water outside is always essential, but watch for freezing.
Treat lawns with anti-tick and -flea preparations and then keep dogs off grass for the recommended time.	When walking in the summer, asphalt and sand can easily burn a dog's paws.	Many dogs are fearful of Halloween, with the constantly ringing doorbell and loud children in strange costumes.	Antifreeze kills dogs. Avoid spillage on your driveway and prevent access to the container in your garage.
After springtime rain, be sure to dry your dog thoroughly, including his feet.	Exercise should be limited to early morning and evening to avoid the hottest hours of the sun.	Dogs can choke on Thanksgiving turkey bones and other treasures they find in the garbage.	Rock salt on sidewalks and roadways can irritate your dog's footpads.
Many dogs shed in the springtime, so spend extra time brushing your dog's coat.	Never leave your dog inside a closed car.	Rodenticides are used often in the fall to keep mice and rats from attempting to enter the home; keep dogs away from these dangerous toxins.	Don't let your dog get too close to portable heaters or fireplaces.
Select a dog-safe mulch for your garden beds.	Fleas and ticks abound: be prepared.	Mushrooms flourish in the fall (and spring), and some can be toxic.	Keep your dogs away from indoor holiday plants.

Dachshund chewing on your rhododendron—he's not going to water it or fertilize it to your satisfaction, and more than likely, he'll get sick. Raise your houseplants on tables and pedestals, far above the Dachshund's ever-flaring nostrils.

In the backyard, there's likely a number of plants, bushes and flowers that can harm your dog. If possible, fence these off so that your dog cannot get to them; otherwise, you'll have to carefully supervise the dog whenever he's in the yard. Dachshunds fancy themselves gardeners, so keep their paws out of your flower beds, no matter how entertained you are by your puppy's dirt-flinging antics. Keep in mind too that some varieties of mulch can make dogs very sick, especially those that include cocoa hulls in their mixtures. A complete list of poisonous plants can be found on the ASPCA's website, www.aspca.org.

Do all you can to keep your ever-curious Dachshund from following his nose into danger.

At a Glance ...

Purchase all of the needed supplies before your puppy steps one paw into the house. Discuss the essentials for your Dachshund, including a crate, food bowls, a collar and leash, a bed, and toys, with your breeder before the puppy comes home with you.

Don't break the bank by purchasing every toy your Dachshund could possibly want to play with. Start out with a small assortment, including a sturdy chew toy, a bouncing ball, and a strong rope toy. Alternate which toys you offer your Dachshund weekly so he doesn't get bored with the selection.

The best way to puppy-proof your home is to get down on all fours and take a look around from your Dachshund's perspective. Chances are, you'll find all sorts of things that your puppy could get into, including dangling wires, old candy wrappers, and hanging houseplants, just to name a few.

Manners Begin at Home

Agood education isn't just for Obedience Trial Champions, it's for every dog. You will appreciate the value of your well-behaved Dachshund's education every time someone compliments you on your dog's sweet temperament and good manners. It's a pleasure to share the company of a happy, mannerly dog.

Don't ever think because your Dachshund is going to be "just a pet" that you have the option of ignoring training. It's for everyone's

Training sessions help reinforce your bond with your Dachshund.

benefit if you train your dog. Your friends and family will thank you for molding your Dachshund into a dog whose company they enjoy. You don't want your dog to be a barking, nipping, whining nightmare. Bad-dog behavior is no fun for anyone, including the dog, and most people will avoid visiting you because of your unruly dog.

Dachshunds are naturally intelligent dogs, sensible and respectful, even if they have a lot of their own strong ideas about the way things should be. A little education early on will pay off in years of good behavior and requires very little time commitment from the owner. Three or four sessions a day, lasting three or four minutes each for a total of about 15 minutes a day, is a small investment. You waste that much time every day flipping through TV channels or playing Words with Friends!

NAME THAT DOG!

Sometimes a dog's name just happens automatically. Some know from day one what they will call their new Dachshund, and others wait a few days to let their dog reveal his personality. It's important to name your Dachshund within the first few days of his coming home, even better if you can decide on his name before you pick him up from the breeder. A purebred dog usually has two names— an official American Kennel Club registration name and a call name (the name you call him around the house). Official dog names usually include the breeder's

Teach your on-the-go Dachshund basic commands, such as to come when called, for both his safety and his good behavior.

Did You Know?

In New York City, few breeds rouse the crowd as much as the Dachshund does at the Westminster Kennel Club dog show in Madison Square Garden, though, to date, no Dachshund has ever gone home with the Best in Show trophy. Dachshunds have won the Hound Group at Westminster nine times since 1930, though many would argue that they have a distinct advantage with three dogs in the Group finals. The smooth Dachshund has claimed the Hound Group First five times.

kennel name along with the puppy's name. Official names are subject to AKC approval and cannot be longer than fifty characters.

The call name is usually a simple one- or two-syllable name that is distinctive and appropriate for the dog. The days of "Spot" and "Rover" are long gone, and many dog owners today prefer "people names" for their dogs. "Helen" and "Fred" are fun names for Dachshunds, unless you prefer to stick with more German names, in which case "Helga" and "Fritz" might be appropriate. Never name your dog anything that rhymes with a command, such as *no, sit, stay,* or *heel.* Hence, Joe, Kit, Jay, and Neal are out!

Among the most popular Dachshund names are Oscar, Frankie, Heinz (tributes to the breed's hot-dog fame), Heidi, Max, Penny, Buddy, and Chloe. Your choice is only limited by your own creativity—perhaps Andy (short for Andouille) or Nobee (short for "no by-products")? Of course, for thousands of options, you can Google "popular Dachshund names" and let the Internet do the job for you!

GETTING TO KNOW YOU

When the new puppy arrives at your home, he will be unfamiliar with the sights, sounds, and smells of his new world and most likely will seem less outgoing and carefree than he was at the breeder's home. Don't rush him. Let him set his own pace for settling in, and be encouraging and affectionate with him. In no time, your Dachshund will soon start to "feel his feet" and begin taking ownership of you and your home.

Puppy Kindergarten

Once your puppy has been vaccinated and is comfortable in your home, enroll him in a puppy socialization class, often called "puppy kindergarten." Puppy kindergarten helps introduce your puppy to other people and puppies, all within a new and strange (but welcoming!) environment. It also gives you a chance to work with a professional dog trainer who will give you tips on how to train your puppy to be a well-behaved member of the canine community. Check your local pet superstore or community center for puppy socialization classes near you.

Begin by getting him used to the members of your family who live in the home. When he becomes comfortable in your home and yard, you will then be able to introduce him to your larger circle of family and friends. Again, don't rush this, as meeting too many new people and experiencing too many new situations at once can be overwhelming. It's always best to allow the pup to settle down at home for the first few days before venturing out.

If you're creative, you'll find that there's a lot you can do at home to have fun with your Dachshund puppy. Don't forget to let him rest between play sessions; just like babies, puppies need plenty of sleep. In addition to games introducing the puppy to his new toys, you can also get started with a little early training. Play a short game of hide-and-seek or fetch with your pup's favorite toy—these games will help your puppy learn his name and to come to you when he is called. Introduce your pup to standing calmly on a table and being gently groomed. This will be helpful on numerous occasions, including your routine grooming sessions and visits to the vet, when it is much easier to deal with a well-behaved dog.

While your puppy is getting used to his new home, make a conscious effort to have him experience the many strange sounds in your house. The idea is to desensitize the dog to noises that he might find scary at first. For example, most dogs perceive the vacuum cleaner as an alien enemy and will bark and even attack it. While your dog is playing with a favorite chew toy, turn the vacuum on so that he hears it. In the kitchen, run the microwave or dishwasher while he's eating his dinner. Give him a treat while the garbage disposal is burping in your sink. In the bathroom, he should hear the toilet flushing, your electric toothbrush vibrating, and your razor buzzing; outside, he should hear the lawn mower revving and the leaf blower whirring. None of these sounds is scary, and that's the message you want to convey to your puppy. Be nonchalant about all of these things, and praise the puppy for playing with his toy or eating his food and not reacting to all the noise. Soon, he'll pay as little attention to your juicer and washer as you do to the grandfather clock that you never hear chime.

Don't be all work and no play! Incorporate fun time into your training sessions as rewards.

FIELD TRIPS

As soon as your Dachshund puppy is confident around the house and is comfortable in your charge, it's time to get him out into the real world for his first field trips. Your puppy will enjoy tagging along to meet new people and see new places.

A treat goes a long way in conveying positive messages to your food-loving hound.

Make Your Puppy a S.T.A.R.

The American Kennel Club has a great program for new puppy owners called the S.T.A.R. Puppy® Program, which is dedicated to rewarding puppies that get off to a good start by completing a basic training class. S.T.A.R. stands for Socialization, Training, Activity, and Responsibility.

You must enroll in a six-week puppy-training course with an AKC-approved evaluator. When the class is finished, the evaluator will test your puppy on all of the training taught during the course, such as being free of aggression toward people and other puppies in the class, tolerating a collar or body harness, allowing his owner to take away a treat or toy, and sitting and coming on command.

If your puppy passes the test, he will receive a certificate and a medal. You and your puppy will also be listed in the AKC S.T.A.R. Puppy records. To learn more about the AKC S.T.A.R. Puppy Program or to find an approved evaluator, check out www.akc.org/puppies/training/index.cfm.

Socializing your puppy during the first eight weeks in your home is critical to his development. It will be fun to introduce the new puppy to your friends and colleagues, and the puppy will enjoy all of the attention showered over him. Showing off your new wiener dog and giving him lots of different experiences helps boost the puppy's confidence in human situations.

Puppies that are not properly socialized during their first sixteen weeks of life may never grow up to be well-adjusted, people-loving dogs. Spontaneous socialization works for some dog owners—if you're the type to visit friends unannounced, take a spin through an outdoor market, or venture into town to window-shop and sip lattes at a dog-friendly café. Other people need more structure and have to plan their outings—if this describes you, commit to taking your puppy to three new locations each week. For example, on Tuesday, plan to go to the local outlet mall or pet superstore; on Thursday, meet a friend and her dog at a local dog park or at an outdoor café for a "yappy" hour; and on the weekend, visit the boardwalk, lake, downtown area, or any place where there will be lots of different people, sounds, and sights.

If you have young children, or if they visit your home frequently, remember to always keep a close eye on any interactions they have with your young puppy. In their excitement, youngsters can easily hurt a small puppy, even with the best of intentions. To make these introductions as pleasant as possible, show the children the correct way to approach and handle a dog. Be sure that the children do not grab at the puppy, pull his ears or tail, or swarm around him. It's best to have the children sit on the floor, near the puppy's level, and allow the puppy to approach them. Dogs do not like to have people reach down over them and pet the tops of their heads. For a low-to-the-ground Dachshund, even a toddler is many times his height. Teach children to allow the puppy to sniff the backs of their hands and then gently scratch under the dog's chin and neck. Even the most reliable puppy will nip at a young person who's not versed in approaching a dog in a correct, unthreatening way.

When it comes to meeting other dogs, Dachshunds are more gregarious than quarrelsome. That's the breed's hound side dominating its terrier side. Nevertheless, always supervise introductions to new dogs. Most Dachshunds are happy to meet other dogs, though they definitely favor other Dachshunds to members of "lesser" breeds. Dachshunds recognize their superiority but will enjoy the company of any dog that agrees that Dachshunds are top dogs. Opposite-sex introductions often go more smoothly than same-sex ones. Males tend to be more territorial when meeting other males; females tend to be temperamental when meeting other females.

When it comes to any other small mammals you may have scampering around your home, your Dachshund will take issue. If you're a rabbit or rat fancier, your Dachshund will view you as a traitor. Dachshunds were bred to exterminate rodents from the landscape, and you're allowing a rat to hide in your basement? Dachshunds categorize rabbits along with all other pet critters, disdaining them equally. If your children keep pet mice, hamsters, gerbils, or guinea pigs, you will have to keep them away from your Dachshund's eyes and nose. There is simply no way to convince a Dachshund that harboring small mammals

Socialization

Socialization is a word that you will hear over and over again from your dog-owning friends, veterinarian, and breeder. It's important to socialize your puppy at a young age, introducing him to an assortment of new people, places, and situations, so that he becomes familiar with the human world around him. Proper socialization will instill confidence in your puppy and will prevent fear and aggression in his adult years.

The Secret of Playtime

Your Dachshund loves to play, and there is no better way to begin training him than during daily playtime with your puppy. Games such as hide-and-seek and fetch will teach your puppy to recognize his name and come when called. Gently roughhousing with your puppy will teach him what is and what is not acceptable when playing with a human. Use playtime as training time, and your puppy will begin to learn the household rules without even realizing it!

is an acceptable pastime. For the sake of your little pets (and your children), do not let your Dachshund make a picnic of Bugs or Mickey.

TAKE THE LEASH

The Dachshund is a free spirit and prefers to live unleashed! If you think that you can take your Dachshund to a large open field, the beach, or a state park and release him to chase the wonders of the outside world, think again or kiss him goodbye! Dachshunds are great wanderers, and they will dart in the direction of a scent faster than the rabbit that left it. All of your dog's schooling will be a fuzzy memory, and soon your dog will be too. Don't let this happen. Always keep your Dachshund on his leash except when he's in your own fenced yard or home.

Accustom your puppy to being on a leash, which can be a strange experience for a tiny youngster. Begin by attaching a simple collar—not too tight, but not so loose that it can get caught on things. Just put it on for a few minutes at a time, lengthening each time period slightly until your puppy feels comfortable in his first item of "clothing." If he attempts to scratch at the collar, distract him by rubbing his chin or the top of his head and initiating a game. Give him a treat, and he'll soon forget about the collar.

After a couple of days, once he is comfortable wearing the collar, attach a small, lightweight leash. The leash you select must have a secure catch yet be simple to attach and release as necessary. Allow the puppy to wander around the house, dragging the leash behind him. He likely won't pay it much mind. That's enough for one day. The next day, attach the leash and let him lead you around the house. You're playing "follow the puppy," and he'll enjoy leading you around as you talk to him and praise him. After a few sessions of this game, you can take the leader role. Encourage him to follow you, offering him a treat as he walks in your direction. Don't pull him; keep it positive and fun. Once you open the door and take him around the block, he will realize that following you around the neighborhood is a lot more interesting than wandering around the kitchen.

Begin training the puppy to walk on your left-hand side. When this has been accomplished to your satisfaction, you can try moving him on your right, but there is absolutely no hurry. If you plan to show your Dachshund, you will generally move your dog on your left.

At a Glance ...

When you first bring your puppy home, let him explore the house (under your supervision!) so that he feels more comfortable. Once he feels more confident around the house, introduce him to the other members of your family, human and furry alike. With proper introductions, your Dachshund will be part of the family in no time.

. . . .

Use games such as hide-and-seek, fetch, and follow-the-leader to teach your puppy a few early lessons. Learning to come when called and being comfortable on a collar and leash are two essential lessons that every puppy must learn.

. . . .

The first sixteen weeks of a puppy's life are the most important for socialization. Your breeder should have already begun introducing your puppy to common household sounds and new people. When the puppy comes home with you, continue the breeder's good work by taking the pup to as many places as you can to boost his courage and instill confidence in the outside world.

House-Training Your Doxie

Dachshunds are just as challenging to house-train as other stubborn hound breeds, thus house-training is a topic that every Dachshund owner dreads. When it comes to house-training any of the hound breeds, it's never a breeze. In fact, the combination of the Dachshund's celebrated nose and that not-so-celebrated stubborn streak makes house-training more of a "gale-force wind" than a "breeze." Your Doxie will challenge your patience, consistency,

Your Doxie will learn to do his business in a spot that you choose for him.

and training techniques. Owners of the strong-minded Dachshund have their hands full.

It's not just hounds, but scenthounds in particular that are the least easy candidates to house-train, and like the noses of his scenthound counterparts, the Beagle and Basset Hound, the Dachshund's snout is an ever-expanding hard drive of information that defies human understanding. Because dog owners have taken to scenthounds such as the Doxie as pets, house-training is a topic that we house-dwelling creatures must contend with. In order to keep a clean, nice-smelling home, humans have to control where and when their pets relieves themselves. Dachshunds, with their flawless noses, will abide by your "clean house" rules as long as you approach the topic the smart way.

The smart way to house-train a Dachshund—meaning the way that works—begins with one simple word: *crate*. Your puppy's crate—big enough for the Dachshund once he reaches his full length—is your best bet for achieving what some Doxie owners have called "the near impossible." The recipe for house-training success also includes three additional and important ingredients: consistency, vigilance, and patience.

STAY POSITIVE

Good-humored owners are often satisfied with a 90-percent success rate—accidents happen to the best of us. While some dog behaviorists and a few doggy psychologists suggest that dogs will pee in the house to be spiteful, in all honesty, potty-challenged Dachshunds aren't trying to get back at you for being out late or not giving them a second treat. Dachshunds simply don't prioritize house-training the way we humans do. Sometimes they forget that there's a preferred place to relieve themselves—preferred in their owners' minds, that is.

Dachshunds are glad that dog trainers no longer recommend scolding puppies for having accidents in the house. What's the point? "Don't yell over spilt piddle" is good advice, and Dachshunds will happily live without any negative consequences for their accidents. After months of accidents, owners will often give up and no longer even attempt to solve house-training problems. Stay strong and consistent, and don't settle for 90 percent or worse.

While you should always praise the dog when he relieves himself in the right (outdoor) spot, you still must make him understand that you're unhappy when he continues to make "mistakes." And the best punishment for a Dachshund who wants to be your twenty-four-hour shadow is to ignore him!

When training any young, intelligent dog, patience is a virtue. Your Dachshund will probably look up at you with that characteristic defiant carriage of the head and those captivating eyes, and you will wonder what he will decide to do next. To obey or not to obey? That is the question. Your pup is certainly capable of being trained, but, if he is to understand what is required of him, you will need to be sensible and consistent in all training. To house-train successfully, you will need to be firm, but never harsh. Use a happy voice for giving praise and a serious tone when giving reprimands.

With any luck, you purchased your puppy from a breeder who began house-training for you. Because crate-training is the preferred potty-training method of most breeders, it's not too uncommon for puppies to have already been introduced to the crate. Some breeders begin crate-training the pups when they are five or six weeks of age. If your puppy has had prior crate-training, by all means, drop to your knees, kiss your clean kitchen floor, and continue it!

Crate Rest

Dachshunds who have been crate-trained love to spend time in their "bedrooms." They are perfectly content and peaceful snoozing away a lazy day. For Dachshunds that are having issues with their backs, veterinarians regularly prescribe strict crate rest. This is no challenge for crate-trained dogs that relish the privacy of their den, but for dogs that are unaccustomed to the crate, it can be stressful to spend hours on end in one. Investing in crate-training pays off in many ways, including possibly the future health care of your dog.

A PIECE OF HISTORY

Europeans developed smaller hounds to suit the needs of huntsmen of their region. While the Germans developed the Dachshund and the Westphalian Dachsbracke, the French bred small hounds that became known as "bassets," with the most popular being the Basset Hound. Other French variations include the Petit Basset Griffon Vendéen, the Basset Fauve de Bretagne, the Basset Bleu de Gascogne, and the Basset Artesian Normand. In Austria, hunters developed the Alpine Dachsbracke; in Switzerland, the Swiss and Jura Neiderlaufhunds; and in Spain, the Sabueso Español.

Doggy Day Care

However, your home is completely different from the one the puppy was raised in. In addition to smelling different, the floor plan, size of rooms, location of doors, and so forth will be all new to the puppy. You must allow the puppy to explore and get used to the area of the house that he will be permitted to live in.

In the first few weeks, limit the puppy's access to one or two rooms (rooms with easily cleaned floors). You don't want the puppy sniffing around in a spare bedroom, trying to find his way to the back door. Make it obvious and easy for your little guy. If you have a large house, it's even bigger to him! He should be able to get to the "potty door" lickety-split, with nary a turn or a second thought. When a puppy has to go, he has to go *now*. A vigilant, smart owner recognizes the signs and gets the puppy immediately outside.

The speed of your house-training success will depend to a certain extent on your living environment and on the season of the year. For all-weather dogs, Dachshunds have real issues with going outside when it's raining (or snowing, or a little too balmy, or misty, or...). Most puppies are perfectly willing to go out into the backyard in dry weather, but when rain is pouring down, many will need considerable encouragement. Likewise, some dogs (especially smooths) disdain the winter months and may be resistant to rough the frigid morning air.

PAPER-TRAINING?

Many owners still ask themselves whether or not they should consider paper-training. For the most part, the answer is no. Most dog owners regard paper-training as nearly prehistoric—just as prehistoric as newspapers themselves! Yes, they (thankfully) still publish the *New York Times*, so for some owners, paper-training remains a viable option. Of course, if you get the *Chicago Tribune* or *Wall Street Journal* on your iPad, that won't help at all! Paper-training was never intended to be a permanent solution, but rather more of a transitional step to outdoor training. For small-dog owners who live in high-rise apartment buildings or who work long hours, however, paper-training may be the best or the only option.

Remember that young puppies have as little control of their bodily systems as babies do—which is to say, virtually none. Peeing is like breathing or scratching to a pup. He doesn't think about it, which means that it's your job to make him think about it. He doesn't quite know why you're so obsessed with his bodily functions, nor does he think it's very natural that you are.

To begin paper-training the puppy, place a thickness of five or six sheets of newspaper or a puppy "pee pad" by the door that leads to the outside. This will teach the pup to associate the paper/pad with going out. When the puppy piddles on "All the News That's Fit to Print," cheer for him like he's your candidate! Praising the puppy makes him think that he did something important, even though he doesn't think peeing is anything worth applauding. Doxies will accept praise for anything—peeing, sitting, or just being cute.

If you plan to transition to an outdoor potty area, progress to taking him outside once he's used to going on the papers by the door. Remember, puppies can't hold their urine the way adult dogs can, and many owners and trainers recommend taking the puppy out hourly—once he's begun circling, sniffing,

and squatting, he won't be able to hold it for a ten-floor elevator ride! Accidents occur because owners aren't paying attention, and usually by the time the puppy is giving his owner a sign that he needs to go, it's too late. You may have only ten to fifteen seconds from the moment he starts to sniff around the floor, wiggle his behind, or whimper. As the puppy gets older, his signaling will start earlier and he'll become more reliable and able to wait until you get him outside.

USING A CRATE

The crate is a natural house-training aid. Your Dachshund puppy is an inherently clean little fellow and he will try hard not to soil his "den" or living space. Thus, his crate is actually a multipurpose accessory: your Dachshund's bedroom within your home, a humane house-training tool, a security measure that will protect your household and furniture when you cannot supervise, a travel aid to house and protect your dog when you are traveling (most motels will accept a crated dog), and, finally, a comfy dog space for your Dachshund when your anti-dog relatives come to visit.

Chances are, you purchased a crate that is big enough to house your Dachshund when he is fully grown. Until he gets to his adult size, you must partition the

It may take some time for you to convince your Dachshund to focus his nose and energy on the task at hand.

crate, giving your puppy just enough room to stand and turn around. If you don't, your puppy will sleep on one side of the crate and relieve himself on the other side. As your puppy (and his bodily control) grows, allow him more space in the crate.

Begin using the crate as soon as the puppy comes home so he learns that this is his new "bedroom." The introduction to the crate can be easily aced with the help of a handful of delicious treats. For the first day or two, toss a tiny treat into the crate to entice the pup to go in. Pick a crate command, such as "inside" or "crate," and use it every time he enters. It is best to give him all of his meals and treats in his crate so that he enjoys being in there and does not feel the need to "protect" his food from others.

You must keep a careful eye on your puppy. Puppies always "go" when they wake up, within a few minutes after eating, after play periods, and after brief periods of confinement. Most of the time, your pup will simply sleep in his crate, so don't put a bowl of water in there with him, or you'll be asking for puddles. At night, don't offer water after 7 p.m. to aid in nighttime bladder control. If he gets thirsty, offer him an ice cube.

Although it may seem like a good idea to use the crate for confinement, never use the crate for punishment. Even if you were sent to your room for misbehaving as a child, this approach does not translate to dogs. Successful crate-training depends on your puppy's positive association with the crate. If the crate begins to represent punishment, he will not associate the crate as his safe place. When the puppy has an accident or is misbehaving, you can whisk the puppy up and place him in his crate, but never do so in an angry fashion or scold him as you put him in the crate. It is better to rush him outside so that he learns to associate the outdoors with elimination.

Another word of caution: do not overuse or abuse the crate. Puppies under three months of age should never be confined for more than two hours at a time unless they're asleep. A good guideline is three hours maximum for a three-month old pup, four hours for the four- or five-month-old, and no more than five hours for dogs six months and older. If you're unable to be home to release the dog, arrange for a relative, neighbor, or dog-sitter to let him out to exercise and relieve himself. Young dogs need to stretch their limbs and exercise to properly develop their muscles, ligaments, and bones. Excessive use of the crate can hinder normal development. It is acceptable to confine a puppy overnight by the time he is twelve months old.

As your puppy matures, his "asking" to be let outside when necessary will become second nature. While your Dachshund pup may take a little longer to house-train, it is rare to have a Dachshund that is unclean in the house. A stud

House-Training Tips

No matter what method of house-training you choose, the ultimate keys to a properly house-trained Dachshund exist within your own training techniques. Your Dachshund looks to you as a leader, and it is important to show your strong-willed puppy that you are the boss through these three training tips.

Consistency: You and your Dachshund speak very different languages. Stay consistent in your house-training rules and habits, and your puppy will better understand what you are asking of him.

Vigilance: An unsupervised puppy is an accident waiting to happen. Until your Dachshund is completely house-trained, stay on him like glue and be sure to take him outside to relieve himself after every meal, play session, and nap.

Patience: Most puppies will not be house-trained in a week. Don't get discouraged, just stick to your house-training techniques. In time, the days of accidents and hourly bathroom runs will be a distant memory. It is best not to trust him out of his crate alone until he is at least one year old; this way, he also avoids many safety hazards and does not damage things by chewing.

dog, however, can be different, for he may well want to mark his territory, and your table and chair legs may be just the places he chooses.

Simple one-word commands are very helpful—"potty" being a favorite—and it seems to work. Never, ever forget to give praise when the deed is done in the desired place. When an accident happens, give your Dachshund a verbal reprimand, but only if you catch him in the act. If you try to reprimand him after the fact, he will simply not know what he has done wrong, which will only serve to confuse him.

It is essential that any messes are cleaned up immediately. If a dog has relieved himself in the wrong place, it must be cleaned thoroughly so as to remove the smell or else he will want to use that particular place again. Do not allow the puppy to watch you clean up. Use a product designed to eliminate, not just disguise, the odor. When your puppy is old enough to be exercised in public places, always carry with you a pooper scooper or small plastic bag so that any droppings can be picked up and discarded.

OTHER CONSIDERATIONS

Remember that puppies need to go out much more frequently than adult dogs do. To be on the safe (and clean) side, take your pup outside every hour while he is awake. Always keep your eyes and ears open, for a youngster will not be able to wait that extra ninety seconds while you gather your sneakers to take him outside. Young puppies will not give you much warning at all, so grab the puppy and race to the door.

Puppy owners should take the puppy out at these crucial times during the day:
- Each time he wakes up from a nap
- Whenever he's released from his crate

You can reward your puppy with some time to explore, but only after he has relieved himself.

- After he's eaten any meal or snack
- After he's slurped a good, fresh drink

Given the Dachshund's strong scenting ability, urinating in the house could also be his way of marking his territory. Dachshunds don't find anything particularly objectionable about the smell of urine—clearly beyond the stench we smell, there's layers of subtle stimulation that only a scenthound can fully understand. Male dogs are more inclined to raise their legs to tell the world "I live here" than females are, even though very dominant females will mark as well. Neutering a male dog will reduce marking behavior in most dogs.

At a Glance ...

Crate-training is the preferred house-training method of most breeders and dog trainers. Your Dachshund will come to treasure his crate as his own private "den" where he can relax and sleep. Keep all associations with his crate positive and stress-free.

· ·

Paper-training is recommended only for those owners who do not have ready access to the outdoors, such as those living in high-rise condominiums or apartments. Whatever method you choose, use the same simple guidelines of consistency and praise.

· ·

No matter how frustrating house-training can be, stay positive with your puppy. With consistency, vigilance, and patience, you and your Dachshund will achieve house-training success, likely in a matter of weeks.

CHAPTER SEVEN

Training the Clever Dachshund

Few sights are more amusing in the obedience ring than watching a Dachshund roll on his back with his feet in the air—the clever Dachshund's version of the three-minute *down* exercise. Sadly for obedience enthusiasts, Dachshunds would rather entertain themselves than follow commands, unless, of course, the mood to obey miraculously strikes them. No one suggests that the breed isn't highly intelligent: many learn commands almost instantly, quickly

grasping the concept at hand (and the treat, too). You're foolish if you think you can train a Dachshund without a handful of tasty treats. The fastest way to the Dachshund's brain is through his nose and stomach! With liver, chicken, or beef, you can motivate your Dachshund to pay attention and heed your lesson plans. Train the dog before dinner because a Dachshund with a full belly is a lazy, sleepy student. With patience, consistency, and effective bribery, there are few things that Dachshunds cannot accomplish.

GETTING STARTED

Puppy kindergarten is done; big-kid Dachshund school starts now. We're no longer playing "follow the leader" or "find the cookie." We are now talking about real homeschooling and actually learning commands. Teaching a dog to respond to basic cues is not only necessary but also highly rewarding. Because the Dachshund is naturally bright, he can be a willing learner. However, you must always be consistent in your approach and remember that this is a fun-loving breed that may not always respond as you expect. However you look at it, some Dachshunds may take more patience to train than some other breeds that are more keen to please.

When his nose is engaged by the scent of a treat, your Dachshund's mind will be focused on you.

Generally speaking, hounds do not accept instruction as eagerly as, say, Golden Retrievers or German Shepherds do. Although some show dogs are trained to perform basic obedience routines, many exhibitors feel that rote training can be detrimental to a dog's performance in the show ring. That said, show dogs are among the most polite of dogs, so their handlers are succeeding in teaching basic good manners. Once a show puppy has learned the basics of standing, staying, and walking attentively on a leash, the puppy can begin to learn other commands. Many show dogs earn the AKC's Canine Good Citizen® award, proving that they're able to obey basic commands.

All training relies on the handler's ability to get and keep the dog's full attention. Dachshunds are always thinking, but not always about the things that you want them to focus on. The breed is easily distracted by the many possibilities he sees, smells, or imagines. The best way to get your dog's undivided attention is with a handful of tasty treats. This positive-reinforcement approach allows the dog to associate treats with praise and thus praise with good things.

Begin training by using food treats, although you will eventually wean your dog off food rewards as he masters each exercise. Praise the dog for a properly executed command before you give him the treat. To wean the dog, begin by skipping the treat reward now and then, but never stop praising the dog. Soon the dog will respond to commands even if he's only getting a treat every second or third time he responds correctly. Remember, though, to never limit your praise.

Always use very simple commands; short, one-word commands are the most effective. Keep training sessions short, so that they do not become too repetitive and thus boring for your dog.

SIT

Most training books start off with the easiest lesson first—*sit*—and this chapter is no different. Although not a critical lesson, the *sit* is a good starting point for training the Dachshund because it is relatively simple, and the success can be rewarding for both dog and owner. The *sit* position is less natural to the Dachshund than to most other dogs because of his body length, so he cannot be expected to sit quite as neatly as would a more normally constructed dog. But this command is easily mastered, even by a distracted Dachshund puppy. You can return to the *sit* exercise at the end of every lesson so that you always end on a positive note.

Take the puppy's leash in your left hand and a tasty treat in your right hand. Allow the puppy to sniff the treat, but do not let him grab it from you. Slowly move the treat over and behind the dog's head and say "sit." As the sight and smell of the treat moves up and over the dog's head, he naturally will sit in order to keep it in view. He can smell that it's still right there! As he adjusts his knees, he will assume the *sit* position. Once this happens, say "good boy" and give him the treat and lots of praise.

If the puppy isn't sitting, begin the exercise again with a new treat. Be patient. Do not push down on the Dachshund's hindquarters, as some trainers might recommend. This is counterproductive with a strong-minded breed like the Dachshund, and pressure on the dog's back is never a good thing.

Pesky Distractions

Doxies have extremely short attention spans due to their scenthound ability to pick up all sorts of scents and distractions from the environment around them. The only way to keep your Dachshund's attention for long enough to train him is to practice, practice, practice. Start out by training in a quiet room in the house away from all other people, sights, smells, and sounds. Keep your lessons short and sweet. Once your Dachshund has mastered the lesson, add a distraction to the mix, such as having a new person come into the room or turning on the television. Keep practicing until your Dachshund obeys the cue despite the distractions around him. Once he's again mastered the lesson, try taking him outside (always on leash) for the ultimate test. If your Dachshund follows your commands among the sounds and smells of nature, you've successfully taught the command!

DOWN

The *down* exercise is not as easy as the *sit*, except when your dog is as low to the ground as the Dachshund. Dogs generally view the down position as a submissive one and feel vulnerable, though this is less of a problem for Dachshunds because they are already accustomed to being at ankle height.

With your Dachshund sitting by your left leg, hold the leash in your left hand and a treat in your right. Place your left hand gently on top of the dog's shoulders (without pushing) and hold the treat under his nose, saying "down" in a quiet tone of voice. Slowly move the treat along the floor, in front of the dog, all the while talking gently. He will follow the food, lowering himself down. When his elbows touch the floor, you can release the treat and give praise, but try to get him to remain in the position for a few seconds before getting up. Gradually, the time of the *down* can be increased.

Can Your Dog Pass the Canine Good Citizen® Test?

An AMERICAN KENNEL CLUB Program

Once your Dachshund is ready for advanced training, you can start training him for the American Kennel Club Canine Good Citizen® Program. This program is for dogs that are trained to behave at home, out in the neighborhood, and in the city. It's easy and fun to do. Once your dog learns basic obedience and good canine manners, a CGC evaluator gives your dog ten basic tests. If he passes, he's awarded a Canine Good Citizen® certificate. Many trainers offer classes, and the test is the "final exam" to graduate. To find an evaluator in your area, go to www.akc.org/events/cgc/cgc_bystate.cfm.

Many therapy dogs and guide dogs are required to pass the Canine Good Citizen® test in order to help as working and service dogs in the community. There are ten specific skills that a dog must master in order to pass the Canine Good Citizen® test:

1. Let a friendly stranger approach and talk to his owner
2. Let a friendly stranger pet him
3. Be comfortable being groomed and examined by a friendly stranger
4. Walk on a leash and show that he is under control and not overly excited
5. Move through a crowd politely and confidently
6. Sit and stay on command
7. Come when called
8. Behave calmly around another dog
9. Not bark at or react to a surprise distraction
10. Show that he can be left with a trusted person away from his owner

In order to help your dog pass the AKC CGC test, first enroll him in basic training classes or a CGC training class. You can find classes and trainers near you by searching the AKC website. When you feel that your Dachshund is ready to take the test, locate an AKC-approved CGC evaluator to set up a test date, or sign up for a test that is held at a local AKC dog show or training class. For more information about the AKC Canine Good Citizen® Program, visit www.akc.org/events.cgc.

Your dog will learn to respond to both the verbal cue and the hand signal for *stay*.

STAY

Stay can be taught with your dog in either a *sit* or *down* position, as usual with the leash in your left hand and the treat in your right. Allow him to lick the treat as you say "stay" while moving from your position beside your Dachshund to stand directly in front of him. Silently count to about five and then move back to your original position alongside him, allowing your dog to have the treat while you give him praise.

Keep practicing the *stay* just as described for a few days and then gradually increase the distance between you. Use your hand with the palm facing the dog in a "stop" sign, indicating that he must stay. Always give lavish praise upon completion of the exercise. Soon, you should be able to do this exercise without a leash (in a fenced area only), and your Dachshund will stay for increasingly longer periods of time. Only attempt exercises off-leash in a securely enclosed area.

COME

Far more important than the *sit* command is the *come* command. Dachshunds are fast little dogs, and they love to run—fast and in whichever direction strikes their fancy. That direction is rarely toward the person desperately bellowing "come!" Experienced dog owners know that teaching the *come* exercise is one of the most challenging, but not nearly as difficult as the "come back!"

Your Dachshund will learn to love to come to you when called. The idea is to invite him to return, offering a treat and giving lots of praise when he does so. It is important to teach the *come* command, for this should incite your dog to run back to you if he is ever in danger of moving out of sight.

You cannot risk failure with the *come* command because it is essential for your Dachshund's safety that he reliably returns to you every time you call him. Thus, you must never call your dog to discipline or scold him. He must always associate coming to you with positive reinforcement—praise, treats, petting, or other positive things.

While you will begin this exercise by using food rewards, you will want to discontinue the use of treats as soon as possible so that your dog will learn to always respond to your call whether or not you have a tasty morsel handy. When

Help Wanted

There is no shame in asking for help. Every Dachshund owner agrees that his or her little dog can be quite a handful at times. If you find yourself struggling to teach your Doxie basic manners, consider enrolling him in a basic obedience class or hiring a professional dog trainer to help get you started and show you the training ropes.

Ask your veterinarian, your breeder, and your dog-owning friends for trainer and class references. Search the Association of Pet Dog Trainers website at www.apdt.com or the Certification Council for Professional Dog Trainers website at www. ccpdt.org. You can also contact the Dachshund Club of America (www. dachshund-dca .org) for advice on how to find a good trainer.

Tricks

The Dachshund is a true clown that may well enjoy learning—or inventing—a trick or two. Which tricks you teach will be a matter of choice, but you must consider that the Dachshund's bodily construction is different from that of other breeds. Start with rolling over, as this is the easiest stunt for every Dachshund to learn and perform.

your Dachshund hears you say, "Ingrid, come" what she's really hearing is "Ingrid, come and get it!" Yes, you are bribing your dog to come to you to get a slice of bratwurst. That's as good an interpretation of reward-based training as any, but sometimes bribery is necessary, particularly when you're dealing with a scenthound that would happily wander away without a moment's thought.

Your Dachshund's immediate response to "come," consistently and without hesitation, can make the difference between your dog's returning to your side and darting into traffic. A reliable *recall*, as the obedience folk call this, is as important as anything you'll teach your dog, and you should put as much energy into it as you do into house-training or leash training. All of the love and bonding you do with your Dachshund will pay off when teaching this command. If your Dachshund is really attached to you and thinks of you as the center of his world, you're in a better position to convince your Dachshund to listen to you instead of following his nose. Never teach the command when you cannot ensure compliance, bringing him back with a long leash. If he learns that you cannot force him to comply, you will have lost the battle with this clever little dog.

Your Dachshund may want to jump or sit up to get a treat or some attention, and new thinking is that this exercise actually strengthens the core muscles and helps prevent back issues.

HEEL

In obedience trials, *heel* is a technical term for walking precisely at the owner's left side under complete control and sitting every time the walker halts. Once your puppy is walking nicely by your side, you can attempt more formal training.

While the dog assumes the *sit* position next to your left leg, hold the loose end of the leash in your right hand and control it lower down with your left. Step forward with your right foot, saying "heel." To begin, take three steps, and then cue him to sit again. Repeat this procedure until he carries out the task without pulling. You can then increase the number of strides to five, seven, and so on. Give verbal praise at the close of each part of the exercise and, at the end of the training session, let him enjoy himself with some free play.

Your Dachshund may not stay focused on you for long, so take advantage of his attention in short training sessions.

At a Glance ...

All dogs respond best to positive reinforcement—praise, petting, and, above all, treats! The best way to train your Dachshund is with a pocketful of tasty tidbits. Eventually, you will wean your puppy off food rewards so that he will perform for vocal praise alone, but until then, bring on the liver!

. . . .

Your Dachshund doesn't have to be an obedience champion, but he does need to learn a few basic commands to be a well-mannered canine citizen. *Sit*, *down*, *stay*, *heel*, and most especially *come* are lessons that all dogs should know, regardless of their breed.

. . . .

Don't hesitate to ask for professional help. Enroll your Dachshund in a beginning training course or enlist the help of a dog trainer. Ask for references from your veterinarian, breeder, or local Dachshund club, or check the Association of Pet Dog Trainers' website at www.apdt.com or the Certification Council for Professional Dog Trainers' website at www.ccpdt.org.

CHAPTER EIGHT

Feed Your Chowhound

Look into the soulful eyes of your Dachshund, and you'll soon believe what he's desperately trying to tell you: *I'm famished*! We are now going to discuss every hound's favorite topic—food!

Even though you'll never convince your Dachshund of this, it requires a fairly small amount of food to keep an active Dachshund going—even a Standard. Your Dachshund will be glad that you're buying the best possible

food available for him, and only a high-quality food in appropriate portions can sustain a healthy, active dog. So how do you select the best high-quality food for your Dachshund? Always begin by finding out what brand of dog food your breeder feeds his or her dogs. If you decide to change your dog's food from the breeder's recommendation, be sure to do so gradually. A puppy's system is delicate, and a sudden change in diet can lead to an upset stomach. Of course, you can always begin by changing the variety of the food you're feeding rather than the brand: try the lamb and rice or the venison and sweet potato flavors to see if your puppy prefers something other than chicken, fish, or beef. You might also try adding a little flavored, low-salt stock to tempt the palate. Regardless, be aware that too many changes and additives can lead to finicky habits, even in Dachshunds, who are notoriously not picky and always hungry.

CHOOSING A BRAND

A visit to a well-stocked pet-supply store will show you just how many brands and varieties of dog food are available. There are dozens of brands, each of which offer multiple flavors and formulas. Likely, there are brand names you'll recognize, and even more that you won't. Large corporations and small mom-and-pop companies alike produce quality products, so how do you choose the best food for your Dachshund? Begin your kibble quest by reading the ingredients label on the package. The ingredients are listed by weight. On a product that's called "chicken dog food," the first ingredient on the list should be chicken—not chicken by-products. "Chicken meal" (or "lamb meal" or "turkey meal") is okay as a second ingredient, but "meal by-products" or "meat meal" is not. *Meal* is a term used for a form of protein that is dried and then ground. How many protein sources are listed before the first fat (chicken fat, canola oil, etc.) on the ingredients list? Four or five is preferable.

Many dog foods contain grains, and you'll see dog-food varieties such as "chicken and oatmeal" or "turkey and rice." Quality grains, such as barley, brown rice, and oats, are welcome additions to the canine diet, but steer clear of foods that include fillers such as rice hulls, soybean meal, or corn bran. Also be aware of any labels that list grains by several different names in order to push them lower on the list, such as cornmeal and corn flour or wheat gluten and wheat bran.

The more natural and recognizable the ingredients, the better. Look for a dog food that doesn't contain artificial colors, flavors, sweeteners, or preservatives. How many preservatives can you name? Likely not many, other than salt (which

Water is as important as any component of a dog's diet and should be available to your Dachshund both indoors and outdoors.

A PIECE OF HISTORY

The beginnings of the Dachshund breed can be traced back to the fifteenth century, from illustrations showing long-bodied dogs with short legs hunting badgers in the countryside. The hounds of medieval Europe were described in texts as having a strong scenting ability with the body type and temperament of modern-day terriers. This description accurately conveys the physical structure and character of the Dachshund today, more than five centuries later.

Natural Diet

Many pet-supply stores are now carrying brands of fresh, natural dog food in the refrigerated section. These foods contain a higher percentage of protein and fewer additives and preservatives. Usually, these foods also contain fewer carbohydrates and starches, forgoing common fillers such as grain and rice. Veterinarians will often recommend a natural diet for elderly dogs or those dogs with grain allergies, digestive problems, or skin sensitivities. Consult your veterinarian if you think your Dachshund would benefit from a change to a natural diet.

isn't good either). Natural preservatives, such as tocopherols (vitamin E) and ascorbic acid (vitamin C), are what you prefer to see instead of scary-sounding abbreviations, such as BHT and BHA, or unfriendly multisyllabic words that you can barely pronounce, such as ethoxyquin, sodium metabisulphite, and menadione. Banned for human consumption by the FDA, menadione, also called vitamin K3 or dimethylprimidinol sulfate/sulfite, is a synthetic version of vitamin K that's not good for dogs either.

Just as your mother encouraged you to eat vegetables at dinnertime, so too should you include them in your dog's diet. Dachshunds can't live on hamburger alone, though they'd like to. If you see peas, carrots, sweet potatoes, or pumpkin among the ingredients, that's a plus, and so are fruits, such as apples, blueberries, and pears.

The Association of American Feed Control Officials (AAFCO) requires that dog foods meet certain criteria to be designated "complete and balanced." For a puppy, the food must have 22 percent protein and 8 percent fat, plus the essential minerals like calcium, phosphorus, iron, and zinc, and vitamins, including A, D, E, niacin, riboflavin, and thiamine. The adult requirements are slightly less at 18 percent protein and 5 percent fat. Talk to your breeder about when to switch your growing puppy onto an adult-formula food. There are also varieties for senior dogs made with fewer calories and additives that benefit aging bodies.

COMMON VARIETIES

The two most common types of dog food are dried (bags or sacks) and wet (canned, resealable bags, or plastic containers), both of which are popular with Dachshunds. Some owners use a combination of the two, though the principal basis of the diet should be the dry product. Adding a scoop or two of wet food to moistened dry product will be appealing to your Dachshund. Read the label, and you will see that wet food is 70–80 percent water and has much lower protein and fat percentages than dry food does.

Should you decide to feed your Dachshund a dry food, be sure to thoroughly read the feeding instructions. For Miniatures, you should choose a dry food described as "small-bite" size. Standard Dachshunds should have larger kibble because chewing more helps control tartar on the teeth; food for medium dogs is the right choice for Standards. Young dogs will appreciate dry kibble soaked in warm water to soften it up a bit. Dry foods should be stored carefully, bearing in mind that its vitamin value declines if not used fairly quickly, usually within about two or three months. If you have a single Dachshund, don't buy a 50-pound bag of dry food because you won't use it up in time.

It is essential that a plentiful supply of fresh water is available for your dog when feeding dry foods in particular, though dogs should, of course, have access to water at all times.

After weaning, a good breeder starts the litter off on a quality puppy food formulated for healthy growth.

Treats

Many owners are tempted to feed their Dachshunds tidbits between meals, but, aside from your judicious use of treats in training, this is not a good idea. Too many treats can cause weight to pile on almost imperceptibly! Be creative when offering your dog treats—baby carrots, unsalted popcorn, and slices of apple or banana will delight many dogs. Crispy raw fruits don't put any weight on the Doxie's frame and are a good way to keep teeth clean and breath fresh.

Some owners prefer to feed fresh foods, but, in this case, owners must be absolutely certain that they are feeding well-balanced diets. There is currently a move toward feeding dogs a more natural diet, similar to what they would eat in the wild. Many say this helps keep teeth clean and breath fresh. Cooked vegetables are also beneficial to this type of diet. Be sure to consult with your veterinarian before deciding to feed your dog a natural, home-cooked diet. Much research and planning go into a natural diet in order to keep your dog healthy and satisfied. A well-balanced vitamin formulated to supplement home-cooked diets is essential. Ask a veterinary nutritionist for guidance.

DINNERTIME!

Your breeder will likely advise you on a feeding schedule. New puppies, ages eight to twelve weeks, will need to be fed as frequently as four times a day. Little bellies can only handle little meals. Once the puppy is three months old, you can feed him breakfast, lunch, and dinner; by six months, you can skip lunch and instead offer a nutritious midday snack. Some owners prefer to feed their adult dogs only once a day, but because Dachshunds prefer to eat in the morning and the evening, it's best to divide their daily portion in half. The twice-a-day rule is good for all small dogs like the Dachshund.

Dachshunds truly love to eat, so you will have to take great care that you do not allow yours to put on excess weight. Extra weight puts additional strain on the heart, back, and joints, and puts a dog under increased risk when under anesthesia.

An active adult dog will require a higher protein content than your typical couch potato (get him off the couch!). As a dog gets older, his metabolism changes, so feeding requirements may change, too. This can mean feeding smaller, more easily digestible portions more frequently throughout the day. By then, of course, you will know your pet well and should be able to adjust his feeding schedule and portions accordingly. If you have any queries, your veterinarian will be able to guide you in the right direction.

At a Glance ...

Combing through the dog-food aisles at your local pet superstore can be overwhelming. Take a close look at the ingredients of your top choices to be sure that a quality protein is the first ingredient listed on the label, that there are natural grains and vegetables included, and that artificial ingredients are limited.

It's best to continue feeding your puppy the same brand and variety of dog food that your breeder was feeding him before you brought him home. If you want to change his food, do so over a few weeks to avoid an upset stomach, slowly mixing the new food with the old until your Dachshund is eating only the new food.

Depending on your Dachshund's age, weight, and lifestyle, there are many varieties of foods to choose from even within your selected brand. Puppies, adults, and seniors all require slightly different formulas, so choose carefully with the help of your veterinarian or breeder.

CHAPTER NINE

Grooming All Three Coats

Dachshunds don't shed as much as many dogs do, and they are pretty clean dogs overall. Owners share that the breed has little doggy odor unless it gets into something truly awful. Hounds do tend to relish rolling in unthinkably pungent stuff, which clearly smells heavenly to them.

Dachshunds are among the few breeds in dogdom that come in three different coat types, so grooming for each variety varies accordingly.

Your Dachshund should at least learn to tolerate the tub. Some Dachshunds love their baths.

Talk to your breeder about the coat care for your particular Doxie. It doesn't take an expert to realize that grooming a smooth Dachshund takes considerably less time than a longhaired or a wirehaired variety, but all three coat types—even the smooth—need regular coat attention. Coat care is an essential part of canine maintenance, and the grooming process should be positive for both dog and owner. Grooming will strengthen the bond between you and your dog if you take care to accustom him to the routine.

Ideally, your Dachshund should be groomed on a firm table with a nonslip surface. A grooming table is a worthwhile investment, especially if you have a wirehaired or longhaired Dachshund. Saving yourself the back pain of stretching and bending down to your Dachshund's level is worth the cost of the table. Dachshund owners choose equipment, such as brushes and combs, that suit them and, of course, their dog's coat type. Your breeder will give you grooming advice when you purchase your new puppy and, as you gain experience, you will develop your own preferences.

COAT CARE

It is essential to keep your Dachshund's coat clean and groom him regularly. How frequently you bathe your dog will depend on his coat type, whether or not he is a show dog, and on his personality—that is, how often he digs and rolls in around the backyard. Exhibitors have individual preferences as to how long before a

show they bathe their dogs, or whether they bathe at all. In the case of wirehaired Dachshunds, bathing softens the coat, so wirehairs that are shown are bathed less frequently than their smooth and longhaired counterparts.

Smooth

Brushing the smooth coat once or twice a week serves to stimulate the coat and rid it of any dead hair. The more of those short little hairs you can remove with a brush, the less you'll have to vacuum around the house. Wipe the nose, eyes, and underbelly with a damp cotton ball or towel to keep them clean, and also gently wipe around the rear end to prevent any buildup of fecal matter.

Some smooth Dachshunds get dandruff, in which case it is wise to add a little extra oil to the dog's diet for a few days; ask the vet about this and any other dietary changes that affect coat condition. Massaging baby oil or almond oil into the coat prior to bathing can also help. An ideal smooth coat has a waxy shine to it, with hair lying flat to the body. Some owners like to use a leather chamois or piece of velvet for a finishing touch.

Longhair

Surprisingly, there are different types of coats among the longhaired variety of Dachshund, and each must be dealt with in the best way for that particular dog. It is essential for a new owner to take advice from those with experience with

Did You Know?

You can add baby oil or bath oil to your Doxie's coat if his skin becomes dry and flaky. Be sure to brush the oil well into the coat and leave it for two to three hours before giving him a good bath. For the longhaired Doxie, follow the bath with a nice crème rinse, always letting it saturate the coat for a few minutes before rinsing thoroughly. Dry thoroughly with a cool dryer to maintain the desired straight longhair coat.

Anal Glands

Located on either side of the anal opening, a dog's anal glands can become blocked from time to time. You will know that your dog is uncomfortable when you see him attempt to drag his rear end across the carpet, the grass, or your furniture. Breeders with know-how can express the glands themselves, but you're better off allowing your veterinarian to evacuate these glands. If done incorrectly, you can hurt your dog; even when done correctly, it's not a pleasant task. Normally, a good diet will help the glands function normally, as firm stools assist in evacuating the contents of the glands with each movement.

longhaired Dachshunds. Longhairs should be brushed every other day with a firm bristle brush, which will remove any mats or tangles as well as any debris in the coat. Any soiled areas of the coat should be spot-washed and dried. In general, longhairs need bathing more frequently than smooths, but still, it is for the owner to decide how often to bathe the dog to retain the best coat quality.

The long coat requires little trimming. Hair growing between the pads of the feet should be carefully trimmed away and the tops of the toes and instep should be tidied up as needed. Any longer hairs that look unsightly can usually be plucked from the coat gently with your thumb and forefinger.

Wirehair

Of the three coat types, the wirehaired variety requires the most grooming. This coat type requires daily attention and, although wirehairs need not be bathed often, their coats will need to be stripped. Stripping is a method of plucking the coat to maintain proper texture. The easiest type of wirehaired coat is what is known as a "pin-wire," which needs much less maintenance, but such coats are few and far between.

Stripping a show dog's coat is usually done with the thumb and forefinger, but pets are often stripped using a stripping knife and scissors. The only way to learn how to strip properly is to watch those who have had much practice. Owners of wirehaired Dachshunds are usually very generous with their advice. As a new owner, you will learn much more from seeing the grooming process in action than you will from reading a book. As with longhairs, it is necessary to remove hair from between the pads of the wirehair's feet when it grows too long.

BATH TIME

Here's a secret about Dachshunds: if you don't bathe them, they eventually are going to stink! That's true not just for Dachshunds, of course, but for any dog that plays and works hard. Nevertheless, Dachshunds don't need frequent baths—once a month is a realistic goal for most owners. And soaping up a little Dachshund takes a lot less time and energy than bathing a Golden Retriever or a gorilla, for example (gorillas definitely smell worse, too!).

Bathing does not remove all of the essential oils from your dog's coat—in fact, bathing does many good things for a dog's coat, such as removing dirt and odor and keeping it looking shiny and resilient; it also keeps the skin pliant and healthy. If a puppy is accustomed to being bathed from a young age, he will be content to accept it as part of his grooming session when he's older.

Grooming Your Dachshund

	SMOOTH	LONGHAIR	WIREHAIR
Pet Grooming	Trim whiskers with straight shears with rounded tips (optional); bathe as needed	Use magnet stripping blade to remove dead hair from back of neck and body; tidy undersides of feet; thin hair on sides of neck; use crème rinse after baths	Clip coat to accentuate desired outline and features (this saves much time, but the desired harsh texture of the wire coat is sacrificed)
Show Grooming	Add baby oil to add luster; trim whiskers (optional); scissor stray hairs on sides of neck; thin underside of tail to give tapered appearance; tidy hair on underside of feet	Use thinning shears to tidy up overly profuse coat on sides and around neck; blend coat on back of thighs; trim hair on feet with straight scissors to give compact, rounded appearance; do not trim tail feathering	Pluck coat with thumb and first finger or strip with specially designed grooming knife (an experienced groomer can demonstrate the proper way to do this from head to foot)

Who doesn't admire the Dachshund's endearing habit of rolling in stinky gunk, remnants of dead worms and bugs, and skunk and deer droppings? Most owners don't understand what makes their otherwise clean hound do the most outlandish, awful things. A dog's desire to "disguise his scent" is linked to his hunting instincts, attempting to lose his scent so that his prey cannot detect him. In a Dachshund's mind, an unsuspecting rabbit will be less alarmed by the stench of a dead skunk than his own aloe and lavender shampoo.

Dog show exhibitors have different rules of thumb when it comes to bathing. Depending on his coat type, a show Dachshund may be bathed before every show weekend. However, for a pet Dachshund, a monthly bath suffices unless he gets particularly dirty or smelly.

EARS AND EYES

When you look into your Dachshund's eyes, you should see nothing more than keen intelligence, a glint of mischief, and unmistakable canine love. You should not see cloudiness, debris, or discharge. Wipe your Doxie's eyes with a soft, moist cloth a couple of times a week to keep them clean and debris-free. They should be clear and bright—if you see cloudiness, blueness, or any sign of injury, such as a scratch, bring this to your vet's attention. A dog can lose his sight quickly if a problem is neglected.

When it comes to your Dachshund's ears, you will better your chances of being heard and obeyed if you keep them clean! Use a moist cotton ball to wipe the interior of the ears once a week. Moisten the cotton ball in an alcohol-free ear-cleaning solution from the pet-supply store. Do not use a cotton swab to poke inside the ear because you could injure your dog. The dog's ear canal is "L" shaped, so you will not be able to reach the lowest region anyway; this is best left to the veterinarian or groomer.

If your dog has been shaking his head or scratching at his ears, there may well be an infection or ear mites present. Likewise, if your dog is carrying his head in a tilted fashion, it also indicates a problem. A thick brown discharge and malodorous smell are also indicative of these problems, and you need to consult your veterinarian right away.

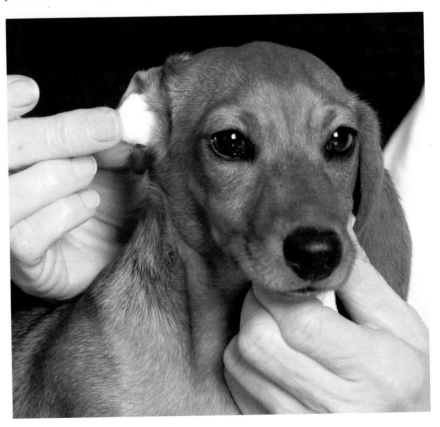

The Doxie's drop ears need regular checks and cleaning to keep them free of debris and infection.

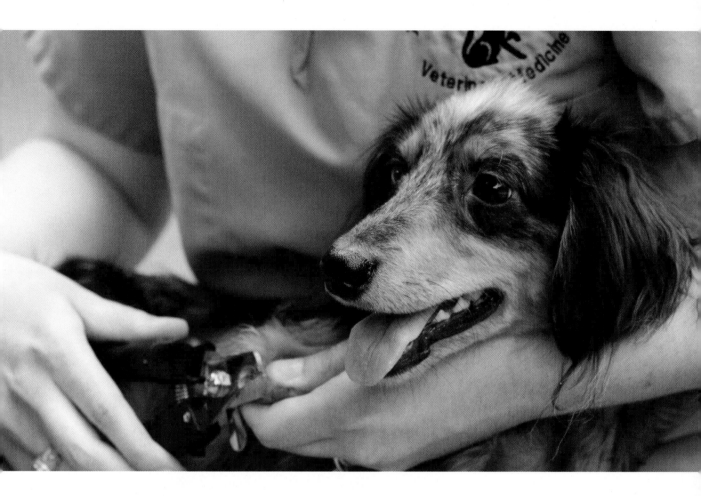

NAILS

Every dog knows that his paws are critical to his survival. A Dachshund can't dig
or run without his feet. Most dogs hate to have their feet touched and will pull
away if you go near those sensitive tootsies, so as soon as your puppy comes home,
begin massaging his feet to get him used to it. While he's lying on your chest
watching TV, hold a foot in your hand and tell him how beautiful his big, round
feet are. Desensitizing the Dachshund to foot handling will eliminate the horrors
of nail clipping later on. A dog that hates having his nails trimmed will be impossible to handle, and Dachshunds are good at keeping their paws to themselves.

You must always keep your dog's nails at a proper length. How frequently
they need clipping depends very much on the surface upon which your dog walks.
Dogs that live primarily on carpet or on grass will need more frequent attention
to their nails than those who regularly walk on hard surfaces. Walking the dog
on the sidewalk or pavement will help wear down the nails, but rarely enough to
eliminate nail clipping altogether. Excessively long nails that are not clipped will
eventually damage the feet, causing the toes to splay. This damage goes right up
the leg and into the shoulder, eventually creating back problems because the dog
cannot walk properly (i.e., on the pads of his feet) if his nails are too long.

If you can get past its name, the guillotine nail clipper is the friendliest device.
Don't be afraid to cut the nails. It's best to follow bath time with nail clipping
because the puppy's nails are soft from soaking in the water. The Dachshund's nails
are dark, which poses a bit of a challenge for trimming. It's impossible to see the
quick, the vein that flows inside the nail. When cut, the quick will bleed, and the

Nail clippers made especially for dogs help you get the job done as easily as possible.

dog may experience discomfort. With dark nails, you're wise to trim only a little bit at a time; even though it may take longer, it's safer than accidentally clipping the quick. Have a styptic pencil or powder handy to staunch the bleeding in case you accidentally clip too close.

Be sure to inspect your dog's feet regularly to be sure that the pads are not cracked and that nothing is wedged or embedded between the toes or pads. Sometimes road tar or other sticky substances can get stuck on or in between the pads, and butter is useful for removal should this happen.

DENTAL CARE

We teach children to brush their teeth two or three times a day as a part of their normal routine. Perhaps our sermon goes something like, "Only brush the teeth you want to keep!" Even though we never say, "Brush those teeth or else you'll die

One type of doggy toothbrush fits right onto your fingertip and is easy to use.

from kidney failure or blood poisoning," that is essentially the message your veterinarian will give to you. Dental problems don't stop inside your dog's mouth. When the gums are infected, all sorts of health problems can arise, spreading through the dog's system and possibly leading to organ failure and eventual death.

It's a lot easier to brush your dog's teeth than to deal with major health problems down the road. Dental cleanliness can be aided by having your dog chew on hard chew toys and feeding him dry kibble, hard treats, and raw carrots. Clean your Dachshund's teeth using a small toothbrush and special canine toothpaste, which you can purchase at your local pet-supply store. The Dachshund has a fairly small mouth, so get an appropriately sized doggy toothbrush. Your dog may not like the procedure at first, but he should easily get used to it if you clean his teeth regularly from puppyhood.

Although your veterinarian will advise you to brush the dog's teeth daily—as you do your own—it may be more realistic to do so every other day or two or three times a week. Don't neglect the teeth, or brushing will become a real chore for both you and your uncooperative dental patient. Be on the lookout for signs of gum inflammation (redness or swelling). If you notice that the gums look red or swollen, a visit to your vet is advised. Keeping teeth in good condition is your responsibility, and you owe this to your dog.

At a Glance ...

All Dachshunds require weekly brushing to keep their coats fresh, shiny, and healthy. Though long-hairs and wirehairs require more upkeep, smooths also need a close eye kept on their thick, flat coat and the quality of their skin.

The Dachshund, due to his relentless ability to dig and roll in the dirt, requires a bath at least once a month to prevent him from exuding that unmistakable doggy odor that Hound owners are so familiar with. After a warm bath, trim your dog's nails and wipe his eyes with a soft cotton ball to keep him in tip-top shape from head to toe.

Don't overlook your dog's teeth. Dental care is extremely important for your dog's ongoing health and well-being. Use a doggy toothbrush and toothpaste formulated for dogs to clean your Dachshund's teeth at least two or three times a week.

CHAPTER TEN

To Your Dog's Good Health

Any breed that can boast a life expectancy of up to sixteen years is one healthy little dog! Generally speaking, small dogs outlive large dogs, and in the case of Dachshunds, Minis have longevity on their side. But, of course, all dogs are different, and good health blesses many a hale and hearty Doxie!

Having taken the best first step—purchasing a sound, healthy puppy from a responsible breeder—your second step is finding a qualified,

reliable veterinarian to care for your dog. Just as a pediatrician plays a vital role in the care of our children, a veterinarian plays a similar role for our pets. A good vet is your "go-to" person whenever you have concerns about your Dachshund's health, and he or she will guide you toward being the best dog owner you can be. Recognizing the signs of good health as well as potential warning signs is the basis of excellent preventive care for your dog.

While spending time with your dog each day, look for the following signs of good health:

1. Moist, black nose, with no crusting or dryness
2. Freedom of movement, with no signs of favoring one side over the other, limping, wobbling, or tentative steps
3. Clean and pink ears, with no discharge, waxy buildup, or foul odor
4. Shiny, resilient coat, clean around the rear and with no indications of parasites
5. Pink gums (no sores), white teeth, and good-smelling breath
6. Bright, clear eyes, with no discharge or cloudiness
7. Eating and drinking normally, with no signs of finickiness, excessive thirst, diarrhea, or bloody stool
8. Overall fitness and good musculature; watch for obesity or weakness

SELECTING A VETERINARIAN

Before you acquire your puppy, you should begin your search for a veterinarian. What qualifications should you consider when selecting a vet? The most fundamental consideration is location. You do not want to select a vet who is a long drive from your home unless there is a good emergency clinic nearby that you can count

CORE Vaccines
Check with your vet, but all puppies should receive vaccines for the following diseases:

CONDITION	TREATMENT	PROGNOSIS	VACCINE NEEDED
ADENOVIRUS-2	No curative therapy for infectious hepatitis; treatment geared toward minimizing neurologic effects, shock, hemorrhage, secondary infections	Highly contagious and can be mild to rapidly fatal	Recommended (immunizes against adenovirus-1, the agent of infectious canine hepatitis)
DISTEMPER	No specific treatment; supportive treatment (IV fluids, antibiotics)	High mortality rates	Highly recommended
PARVOVIRUS-2	No specific treatment; supportive treatment (IV fluids, antibiotics)	Highly contagious to young puppies; high mortality rates	Highly recommended
RABIES	No treatment	Fatal	Required

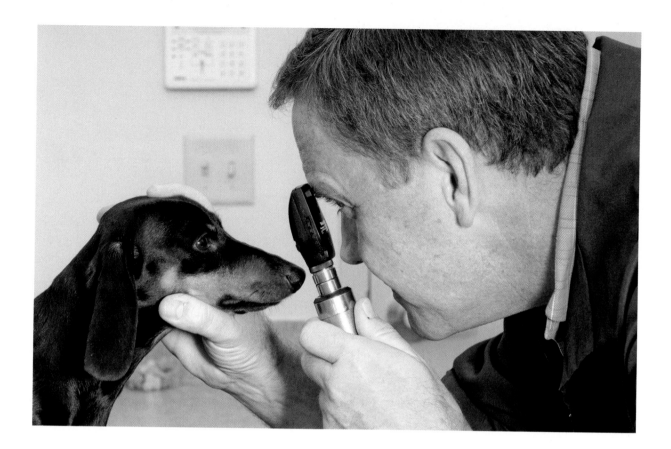

on for the unexpected. Of course, you may have fewer options if you live in a rural part of the country, in which case you'll also have to make sure that your chosen veterinarian is experienced in companion animals and not just large farm animals. There are few similarities between Miniature Dachshunds and horses!

A good vet will be as concerned about your Dachshund's health as you are.

If you have trusted dog-owning friends and acquaintances, ask them for recommendations. They will be able to tell you more about the vet and his or her office than you'll be able to find out with a single visit. How easy is it to get appointments? How flexible are the hours? Is the vet friendly and personable? Does he or she speak in language that's understandable to people without a medical degree?

A PIECE OF HISTORY

In the early days of the Dachshund breed, the little hound was used for hunting both larger game, such as badger and boar, and smaller game, such as fox and rabbit. From this hunting necessity arose two different sizes of Dachshund, those weighing 30–35 pounds and those weighing 16–22 pounds. These sizes have evolved into present-day sizes of 16–32 pounds for Standards and under 11 pounds for Miniatures. Dachshunds who fall in between those ranges are fondly, but not officially, called "tweenies." Records of both breed sizes date back to 1885, and while the Dachshund Club of America has existed since 1885, Dachshunds—despite their ground-hunting skill—were not added to the AKC field trial events until 1935.

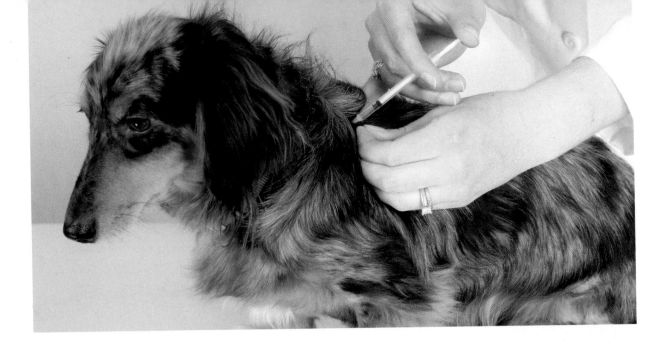

References are also extremely valuable, as is a little research. Contact your state's veterinary medical board to confirm the vet's certification and the American Animal Hospital Association (www.aahanet.org) to find out if the clinic is certified. It's a bonus if the veterinarian's practice is listed on the AKC website as a member of the AKC Veterinary Network (www.akc.org/vetnet) as well.

When you visit the vet's office for the first time, be observant of the cleanliness and general feeling of the facility. Is the office modern and sleek or warm and inviting? Is the clinic busy? Are the receptionists welcoming and helpful? Do you get a good feeling from the vet techs? Don't be shy about asking about the payment policies. Inquire about fees, billing policies, credit cards, and pet insurance.

Spend time talking with the veterinarian to decide whether you like his or her approach. If you already have your puppy, watch and see if the veterinarian is interested in you and your new Dachshund or if he or she seems aloof and removed. How does he or she interact with the dog? A dog's instincts may be better than your own, though it's not uncommon for puppies to act shy or timid in strange environments. Your little angel puppy may even transform into a tyrant as soon as you walk into the waiting room. On that note, it's best to take your Dachshund to the veterinarian's office in his crate. He will be safer and more content, and you can avoid interactions with strange dogs.

Find out if the practice offers other services, including grooming and boarding. Do they have after-hour care or emergency services? If it's a large multiple-vet facility, you may be fortunate to have specialists on the premises. They also may have specialized equipment, although be wary of any vet who wants to do advanced tests prior to basic bloodwork or a simple X-ray. A good rule of thumb is to do tests in order of price: a $60 blood workup should definitely be done before a $2,000 EKG.

VACCINATIONS

Breeders should make sure that puppies receive their first set of inoculations at around eight weeks of age. Upon purchasing the puppy, the breeder will give you a record of which shots the puppy has received and when the booster shots are due. At your pup's first visit to the veterinarian, the vet will give the puppy a thorough exam to make sure that he's in good overall health, including a check of his heart, lungs, coat, mouth, and general condition. The vet will check the puppy's ears for mites, which are common in young pups. Take along a stool sample so the vet can check for internal parasites such as roundworms or hookworms. Parasites can sometimes be transferred to puppies by their mother, though breeders should always worm puppies prior to sale unless they have negative fecal exams.

The initial vaccination schedule continues until the pup is about sixteen weeks old, after which the dog needs only boosters on a schedule set forth by your veterinarian. Discuss with your vet which vaccinations he or she feels are required. This will depend on where you live, how frequently your dog encounters other dogs, and so forth.

The American Veterinary Medical Association (AVMA) recommends four *core* vaccines, all of which are highly recommended to protect canines against dangerous,

Other Vaccines and Treatment

Depending on where you live and your dog's needs, the following ailments and diseases can be treated through your veterinarian:

CONDITION	TREATMENT	PROGNOSIS	RECOMMENDATION
BORDETELLA (KENNEL COUGH)	Keep warm; humidify room; moderate exercise	Highly contagious; rarely fatal in healthy dogs; easily treated	Optional vaccine; prevalence varies; vaccine may be linked to acute reactions; low efficacy
FLEA AND TICK INFESTATION	Topical and ingestible medications	Highly contagious	Preventive treatment highly recommended
HEARTWORM	Arsenical compound; rest; restricted exercise	Widely occurring infections; preventive programs available regionally; successful treatment after early detection	Preventive treatment highly recommended; treating an infected dog has some risks
INTESTINAL WORMS	Dewormer; home medication regimen	Good with prompt treatment	Preventive treatment highly recommended
LYME DISEASE (BORRELIOSIS)	Antibiotics	Can't completely eliminate the organism, but can be controlled in most cases	Vaccine recommended only for dogs with high risk of exposure to deer ticks
PARAINFLUENZA	Rest; humidify room; moderate exercise	Highly contagious; mild; self-limiting; rarely fatal	Vaccine optional but recommended; doesn't block infection, but lessens clinical signs
PERIODONTITIS	Dental cleaning; extractions; repair	Excellent, but involves anesthesia	Preventive treatment recommended

Your Dachshund trusts you to provide for his good health and well-being.

potentially deadly, diseases. Canine distemper, canine parvovirus, canine adenovirus (type 2), and rabies are all highly contagious diseases that affect both puppies and adult dogs. While none of the core vaccinations should be considered optional, rabies immunization is required by law in all fifty states. Most municipalities will not issue a dog license without proof of a current rabies inoculation.

Noncore vaccines, recommended by the AVMA only in particular circumstances and regions where risk is believed to be present, include measles, *Bordetella bronchiseptica* (commonly known as kennel cough), canine parainfluenza virus, canine influenza virus, leptospirosis, canine coronavirus, and Lyme disease (borreliosis). Your veterinarian will advise you on which of these inoculations you should consider for your Dachshund based on where you live and your dog's lifestyle.

The AVMA recommends that veterinarians vaccinate adult dogs every three years instead of annually, although the rabies vaccination is regulated by state laws and is often required yearly. Your veterinarian will know your local requirement. Your vet will also advise you on the best vaccination schedule for your Dachshund, helping you stay up-to-date on required boosters. However, it is completely your responsibility to get your dog to the vet in a timely fashion. Beyond a postcard or telephone call to remind you what shots are due, the vet has no further obligation. For the continued safety and health of your dog, keep his shots current.

QUIT BUGGING ME!

While grooming your dog, always be on the lookout for fleas and ticks or the remnants of these unwanted parasites. It can be upsetting to watch your Doxie scratching at his midsection or biting at his flank in pursuit of an itchy flea. It's more than upsetting to your dog—it's bothersome and potentially painful. Parasites can devastate your dog's coat and turn his skin into a bleeding, scabby mess. Fortunately, there are many effective parasite preventives on the market, but if you spot a flea or tick on your dog or see tiny black droppings, it's time to don your battle gear.

Dog owners have been waging war on fleas and ticks for hundreds of years, and the bugs have been winning until modern times. Thanks to advances in chemical and biological science, we now have the means to completely eradicate parasites from our dogs' coats, ears, bloodstreams, and hearts.

Fleas often arrive without warning and in force on your dog's coat, but luckily, they are easy to deal with. Your veterinarian will provide a prescription flea

Cancer

A dreaded disease in humans and dogs, cancer can take many forms in canines. Research shows that approximately 41.5 percent of dogs will encounter cancer in one form or another. Hemangiosarcoma, a relatively common malignant tumor of cells, is often noticed as bumps on the skin, but the cancer often metastasizes before the lumps are discovered. Fortunately, Dachshunds aren't more prone to cancer than other breeds of dog, but your vet should still do regular all-over checks of your dog to catch any abnormalities as early as possible.

Support Canine Health Research

AMERICAN
KENNEL CLUB™

The mission of the American Kennel Club Canine Health Foundation, Inc. (AKC CHF) is to advance the health of all dogs by funding sound scientific research and supporting the dissemination of health information to prevent, treat, and cure canine disease. The foundation makes grants to fund a variety of health efforts:

- **Identifying the cause(s) of disease**
- **Earlier, more accurate diagnosis**
- **Developing screening tests for breeders**
- **Accurate, positive prognosis**
- **Effective, efficient treatment**

The AKC CHF also supports educational programs that bring scientists together to discuss their work and develop new collaborations to further advance canine health.

The AKC created the foundation in 1995 to raise funds to support canine health research. Each year, the AKC CHF allocates $1.5 million to new health-research projects.

How You Can Help: If you have an AKC-registered dog, submit his DNA sample (cheek swab or blood sample) to the Canine Health Information Center (CHIC) DNA databank (www.caninehealthinfo.org). Encourage regular health testing by breeders, get involved with your local dog club, and support the efforts to host health-education programs. And, if possible, make a donation.

For information, contact the AKC Canine Health Foundation, P.O. Box 900061, Raleigh, NC 27675-9061 or check out the website at www.akcchf.org.

Health Insurance

Because life is filled with unexpected surprises—some not so welcome—it's best to be prepared. The time to invest in health insurance for your Doxie is when he's a puppy. There are many excellent providers in the marketplace, and you can purchase the plan that is right for you and your budget. At the very least, you want a policy that will cover emergency care and major health issues. No one wants to make life-and-death decisions about his or her dog based on financial considerations. Visit www.akcpethealthcare.com to learn more about PetProviders, the health insurance company that has been working directly with the AKC since 2003.

remedy either in pill form or in a liquid form that you squeeze between your dog's shoulder blades once a month or so to kill existing fleas and prevent future infestations. Once you've taken care of the fleas on your dog's body, don't forget to address your home. Fleas can live for months in your carpet, on your couch, or in your dog's bed. Vacuum and spray indoors thoroughly with a safe insecticide, and if the problem is bad enough, "bomb" the house with a stronger formula designed to kill adult fleas and the immature forms of eggs, larvae, and pupae.

Ticks are usually less of a nuisance than fleas, and they are larger and easier to spot burrowing into your dog's skin. If you do find a tick on your dog, remove the tick carefully and completely with a set of tweezers, and watch the site over the next few days to be sure it doesn't become infected or inflamed. In some areas of the country, ticks are known to carry diseases such as Lyme disease (borreliosis), Rocky Mountain spotted fever, Colorado tick fever, and ehrlichiosis. Your veterinarian may suggest a few extra vaccines to protect against these diseases if you live in these tick-prone areas.

Mites are another type of external parasite that can infest our pets. The most common mite found on dogs is the pesky ear mite. These super-tiny bugs cannot be seen with the naked eye, though smelly, itchy ears and signs of brown discharge are all the evidence you need to know that a mite infestation is present. You can purchase an ear-mite solution from your veterinarian to treat the problem.

Internal parasites, even more deadly than the itchy external ones, include various types of worms. The most common is the roundworm. Less frequently encountered, tapeworms can be even more debilitating. Your vet will examine your dog's stool sample for signs of worm infestation. Perhaps the most serious are heartworms, which are transmitted by infected mosquitoes, so if you live in a heavily wooded area or near a lake or pond, you should be especially conscientious about protecting your dog. If you're constantly being bitten by mosquitoes while sitting in your backyard or on your front porch, your dog is suffering too. Thanks to monthly preventives, though, heartworm is not as common as you might think. Discuss the necessity of heartworm preventives with your vet and get his or her advice about the best option for your Dachshund. Your vet will check your dog for heartworm (and other worms) prior to beginning any ongoing regimen.

SPAYING AND NEUTERING

The decision of whether or not to spay or neuter your dog is an easy one. The facts are straightforward and convincing, and the American Kennel Club believes that spaying or neutering is the most responsible choice for pet owners. If you do not plan to show or breed your Dachshund, spay or neuter him or her.

Your Dachshund's regular physical exam will include a full hands-on body check for lumps, bumps, symptoms of parasites, or other signs of problems.

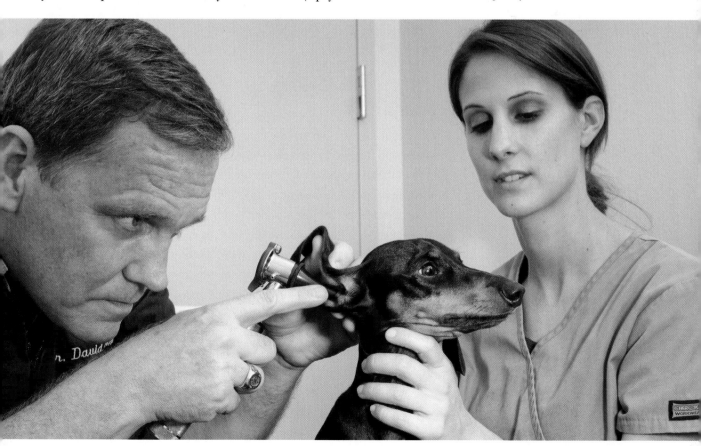

Heatstroke

For heatstroke, cool (not cold) water must be applied immediately, especially over the dog's shoulders; in severe cases, the dog's entire body should be wet down with a hose or running water. Dogs can die quickly from heatstroke, so urgent veterinary attention is also of paramount importance. Conversely, in the case of hypothermia, keep the dog warm with hot-water bottles and give a warm bath if possible.

Many responsible breeders require puppy owners to have their pets spayed and neutered, and they will include this stipulation in their sales contracts.

The surgical procedures for spaying a female dog (removing the uterus and ovaries) and neutering a male dog (removing the testicles and spermatic cords) are routine surgeries for most experienced veterinarians. While there is risk with any kind of surgery, the procedures are not considered dangerous, and dogs recover completely within a few days to a week. Females usually require more time to recover from their surgery, which is technically a hysterectomy.

Spaying or neutering does not alter a dog's personality, though it does discourage male dogs from straying when they smell a female in season. Some Dachshund owners also succumb to the myth that spaying and neutering will cause the dog to gain weight. It's not the lack of a uterus or testicles that causes a Dachshund to gain weight, it's too many calories and too few laps around the neighborhood.

Avoiding unwanted litters should be enough inspiration to spay a female, and the chances of your Dachshund accidentally being bred by another purebred

Dachshund are pretty slim. More than likely, you'll be contending with an unfortunate pairing, and trying to sell a litter of ten Dachshund-Dalmatian puppies or Doxiepoos is a feat you want to avoid!

There are real health advantages to spaying and neutering as well. Statistics show that spayed females live longer, healthier lives compared to their unspayed counterparts, and that neutered males exhibit a lower risk of prostate cancer. Of course, neutered males are completely free of testicular cancer, as well. No male or female should be neutered or spayed before reaching adulthood to allow proper growth and development that come from hormones.

INTERVERTEBRAL DISK DISEASE (IVDD)

The Dachshund, due to his extra-long construction, is more predisposed to this neurological problem than any other breed. The breed's *chondrodystrophic* structure, defined by a normal-sized body and very short legs, poses a threat to the dog's neck and back. The intervertebral disks serve to stabilize the dog's spine, acting a bit like shock absorbers.

Dachshunds and other long-backed dogs are prone to a form of the disease known as Hansen Type 1 IVDD, which is commonly referred to as "ruptured disks" and is most often seen in young to middle-aged dogs. The rupture, characterized by an extrusion in the spinal column, comes on quite suddenly, and affected dogs may lose movement in both hind legs or walk with a wobbly gait. Veterinarians often recommend a type of surgery called disk fenestration as the best course of treatment for this type of IVDD.

If your Dachshund is showing signs of impaired movement, there is no time to waste. Gently place him in his carrier and take him to the vet's office. The faster you recognize the symptoms and act, the better the likely results. This is a very painful condition, even though Dachshunds tend to be more stoic than other dogs. Some vets choose to act more conservatively at first, prescribing steroids and strict crate rest for four to six weeks. Physical therapy has also helped Doxies regain their ability to walk once affected by IVDD.

At a Glance ...

Find a good veterinarian before bringing your puppy home from the breeder, and be sure that you are comfortable with his or her bedside manner and office practices. Your veterinarian will act as a resource to you throughout your Dachshund's life, so your choice of vet is an important one.

. . . .

The American Veterinary Medical Association (AVMA) recommends an assortment of core and non-core vaccines for pets in the United States. Although core vaccines are recommended as essential for all dogs, noncore vaccines are suggested for dogs that live in certain regions of the country where there is an increased risk of exposure to certain diseases.

. . . .

Preventive health care is the most effective health care. Keep a close eye on your Dachshund for any physical or behavioral symptoms that seem out of the ordinary. When in doubt, call your veterinarian for help. The sooner you address the health issue, the more effective the treatment will be.

CHAPTER ELEVEN

Keep Your Doxie Active

Originally bred to chase down wild animals such as rabbits and badgers, the Dachshund is a tough little dog with surprising endurance. Most Dachshunds today spend their lives rather quietly, with daily walks around the block being their most exciting adventures. Rarely do modern-day Dachshunds get the opportunity to barrel down a hole in pursuit of a frenzied badger, so if your dog is not a hunter or competition dog, be mindful of how much

exercise your Dachshund is getting. The Dachshund doesn't need to be walked eight times a day or go for hikes of three or four miles—such a regimen would be welcome for a Border Collie or Greyhound but is overkill for a Doxie. A couple of half-mile walks a day will keep your adult Dachshund in shape, both physically and mentally, although that is too much exercise for a puppy.

Be mindful that you don't overdo your Dachshund's exercise on the weekends. Like people, dogs need regular exercise, not a weekend fitness blitzkrieg. Don't expect your weekday couch potato to transform into a weekend warrior. Though you'll likely have more time on the weekends for activities, it isn't fair or healthy for the dog to engage in intense, once-a-week exercise.

Just as you would be sore if you only went to the gym once a week, the effects are the same on an otherwise sedentary dog. The solution is to work short periods of exercise into your daily routine. Walking is a no-brainer, and daily walks at a brisk pace will do you both lots of good. Because you need to take the dog outside several times each day to do his business, make a point of spending ten extra minutes after potty trip to take a lap or two around the block. You'll be surprised at how the added activity will benefit your Dachshund, and it will make you feel better, too!

Aside from walking, there are a number of other activities you can engage in that are both healthy and fun. Fetching games, using a Frisbee, a ball, or any other toy, is exciting for your Dachshund and good cardiovascular activity for you. Rabbit-loving Dachshunds instinctively love to chase, so a simple game of fetch will not only be good exercise for your dog but also harken back to the breed's roots. It may take some training to get your dog to return the ball or Frisbee to you, though, because "release" is not part of a Dachshund's vocabulary. He's not a retriever like a Golden or a Labrador. However, if you add praise and an occasional treat to motivate your dog, your Dachshund will be fetching and retrieving in no time.

It's worth mentioning that exercise also pays off in your Dachshund's continued good health. The breed is prone to obesity and subsequent back problems, and the best way to avoid these problems is to keep your dog trim and active.

Now let's get out of your backyard and explore the many rewarding activities offered by the American Kennel Club. In addition to the AKC's signature event, conformation (more commonly known as *dog shows*), the club also hosts companion events, such as obedience and agility trials, as well as performance events.

A hunter by nature, the Dachshund can participate in earthdog tests and Dachshund field trials, but he's also adaptable enough to participate in other AKC events, including agility and obedience trials, Rally, and lure coursing. Make the most of your Doxie's people-loving character and get your dog involved in canine therapy work as well.

DOG SHOWS

Any purebred Dachshund that has not been spayed or neutered can participate in a dog show, but it takes a special kind of dog to really show. A winning Dachshund possesses natural showmanship, the chutzpah to get out in the ring and strut his stuff. Your Dachshund should be completely socialized and in good physical shape—trim and well conditioned.

The first step toward getting involved with dog shows is to visit one. Visit the AKC website (www.akc.org) to find an event in your area. Dog shows vary in size—from small local shows that attract a few hundred dogs to large outdoor events that feature thousands of dogs. There are also specialty shows for Dachshunds only; these are regional specialties held by regional clubs and an annual national specialty held by the Dachshund Club of America. You can visit most outdoor dog shows with your dog, but check beforehand to be certain.

Once at the show, be sure to purchase the show catalog so that you know where and when the Dachshunds will be judged. You can learn a lot about dog shows simply by watching the judging procedure in the ring. Dogs sorted by "class" have not yet won championships, and they are usually divided by age and sex. Regular classes include the Puppy Class (six-to-nine-month and nine-to-twelve-month), the Twelve-to-Eighteen-Month Class, the Novice Class (for dogs one year of age and older), the Bred-by Exhibitor Class, the Amateur-Owner-Handler Class, the American-Bred Class, and the Open Class. Aside from these and other regular classes, there is Beginner Puppy Competition for puppies at least four months old but less than six months old on the day of the event.

Dachshunds are divided by coat type (variety), not size, with the smooths, wirehairs, and longhairs competing separately. The Best of Variety of each coat type proceeds to the Hound Group competition, where they compete with the Best of Breed winners from all of the other Hound breeds. The dog that places first in the Hound Group then competes with the other six Group Firsts (from

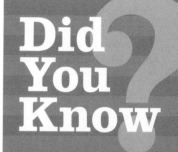

Did You Know?

The first Dachshund to earn a Triple Championship title was CT DC Sadsack The Cupid Clone MW ME, a female wirehaired Miniature Dachshund whose accomplishments were in tracking, conformation, and earthdog tests. The title was achieved on April 19, 2002. She was owned by Lois Ballard.

The elegant longhaired Dachshund is an impressive sight in the show ring. Doxies of all coat types and varieties are crowd favorites at dog shows.

the Sporting, Working, Toy, Terrier, Non-Sporting and Herding Groups) for Best in Show.

Dogs are judged based on how well, in the judge's opinion, they conform to the breed standard. In order to become a champion, the dog must win a total of fifteen points under three different judges; the points are determined by the number of dogs competing. A three-, four-, or five-point win is called a major, and two majors are required under different judges. Visit www.akc.org and click on "Conformation" under "Dog Shows and Trials" for more information.

OBEDIENCE

Open to all dogs, obedience trials have been offered by the AKC since the 1930s and remain popular events around the United States. Dogs are scored by judges on their ability to execute a series of exercises. There are three levels of competition in obedience: Novice, Open, and Utility, in which dogs can earn the Companion Dog (CD), Companion Dog Excellent (CDX), and Utility Dog (UD) titles respectively. To earn a title, a dog must win three legs in competition (a leg is a score of no less than 170 out of 200 points in which the dog earns more than half of the points offered for each exercise). In each level, the exercises become increasingly difficult, from a one-minute sit and heel on leash in the Novice level to a dumbbell retrieve over an obstacle and scent discrimination in the Utility level.

Dachshunds aren't natural obedience dogs, but dedicated handlers who have patience and a good mentor can absolutely succeed. To date, five Dachshunds have won the ultimate obedience title, OTCH (or Obedience Trial Champion). The most recent was OTCH Victory's Emilie der Lump W UDX in 2002.

For more information about obedience trials in your area and how to get involved, visit www.akc.org and click on "Obedience" under "Dog Shows and Trials."

AKC RALLY®

Rally® began as a separate AKC event in 2005 and, though exciting and fun as an event in itself, it's also a great stepping stone from the AKC Canine Good Citizen® (CGC) program to the world of obedience and agility. Like in obedience trials, the dog is judged on each exercise, but precision is not as important. Divided into three classes, Novice, Advanced, and Excellent, Rally is a timed course of ten to twenty stations. Each station is marked by a sign describing what's required for the dog and handler to do, such as "left turn," "360° right," "fast pace," and "offset figure 8." There are currently 299 possible signs!

The judge designs a unique course for each trial, and participants are given a map of the course to review and walk-through before competing. Handlers can communicate with their dogs using voice and hand signals but are not allowed to touch their dogs. In order to gain a title, the dog must earn three legs (scoring 70 out of a possible 100 points) under two different judges. Four titles are offered: Rally Novice (RN), Rally Advanced (RA), Rally Excellent (RE), and Rally Advanced Excellent (RAE). A dog must be six months or older to participate.

Visit www.akc.org and click on "AKC Rally ®" under "Dog Shows and Trials" to learn more about this fun and exciting sport.

AGILITY

Although a fledgling sport compared to obedience, agility has taken off like a peregrine falcon to become the AKC's most popular companion event. A fun-filled obstacle course for dog and handler, agility is as much fun to watch as it is to participate in. And it's even more fun when there's a Dachshund in the ring!

Essentially, agility is an obstacle course for dogs in which the dog and handler are judged on both speed and accuracy. Truly a team event, agility has become an infinite dog sport with many different classes and too many titles to list.

Dachshunds and their handlers face many "obstacles" in agility beyond the actual jumps, poles, and tunnels. Let's face it, this long and low breed was not designed to run and jump and weave. Agility—unlike tracking, earthdog tests, and field trials—is not a nose sport, so Dachshund handlers have to work against the dogs' natural tendency to sniff and to keep their dogs' noses off of the ground. The breed is very easily distracted by smells in the grass and movement that catches their eye, so handlers have to be diligent to keep the Doxie on course. Keep in mind, too, that a Dachshund can barely see your knees when he looks up at you, so hand signals have to be larger and lower.

Agility jumps are a serious consideration for Dachshunds. Only lean, muscular dogs that are accustomed to regular exercise should participate in agility. When training your Dachshund for jumps, start with very low jumps and train together for at least six months to condition the dog for higher jumps. Low-jump training reduces the impact on a Dachshund's back and joints and helps to develop muscles and bones. A Dachshund needs additional strength in his skeletal frame and musculature to withstand the impact of landing on all four feet.

The weave poles tend to be the most difficult obstacle in an agility course, since the Dachshund is driving a longer truck than other dogs and maneuvering around the poles is not a natural canine behavior in the first place.

Nonetheless, agility has become popular among Dachshund enthusiasts, and it's not uncommon to see the breed competing and winning in the ring. There have been more than two dozen MACH Doxie winners—the Master Agility Champion title is the most difficult of all titles to achieve—as well as five PACH (Preferred Agility Champion) winners. Dogs must be at least one year of age to participate in agility, as the obstacle course is too demanding on the developing bodies of puppies.

Visit "Agility" under "Dog Shows and Trials" at www. akc.org to learn more.

TRACKING

Dachshunds excel in all nose sports, and tracking is all nose! A Dachshund and his handler must follow a scent trail that was laid the day prior in search of an object. With the dog in a harness on a long leash, the handler follows his dog over a track that can range from 440 to 1,000 yards in length, from thirty minutes to five hours old, with three to eight directional changes. On the most difficult tracking tests, dogs encounter various terrains, roads, water sources, and urban areas. Titles include Tracking Dog (TD), Tracking Dog Excellent (TDX), Variable Surface Tracker (VST), and Champion Tracker (CT).

Dachshund puppies can begin tracking training as soon as they leave their dams (mothers). Dachshunds love to receive treats for following their nose—what could be easier? Trainers usually begin by hiding a favorite toy in the backyard, and letting their puppy seek it out on a long leash. Don't hide food because a tracklayer is never going to leave a chicken leg for your dog to find. Never use a flexible, retracting leash because any sudden jerking of the leash will distract the puppy and take him off his track. Vary locations for your practice sessions, and don't attempt the exercise more than twice a week. Visit the AKC website at www.akc.org/events/tracking or the DCA website at www.dachshund-dca.org for detailed information about getting involved in tracking tests.

EARTHDOG TESTS

Earthdog tests are designed to gauge the natural hunting aptitude of a Dachshund or small terrier. The tests are not competitive like field trials but instead offer a simulated hunting experience for the dogs. Beginning with den work and quarry, the earthdog program tests the dog's willingness to locate and work its quarry underground. Visit the AKC website at www.akc.org/events/earthdog to request a copy of the AKC's rulebook for earthdog tests and to find a club that sponsors tests near you.

In the first test, Introduction to Quarry, the Dachshund is tested on his willingness to follow the quarry's scent to the entrance of the den, enter it, and engage the quarry by barking, digging, growling, lunging, and biting at the bars of

With his low-to-the-ground body and his ever-sniffing nose, the Dachshund is a natural tracker.

the rat's cage. To prepare for a first earthdog test, encourage your Dachshund to sniff at the scent of a passing rabbit or squirrel. When you see a squirrel scamper by your path on a walk, head in the direction of the "quarry" and pat the ground to coach your dog to follow the scent.

Once your dog readily begins to sniff and follow the squirrel's or rabbit's scent line, you can start training him to follow a scent into a tunnel. You can either use wooden liners or a mini-maze of cardboard boxes set up in your backyard. Your goal is to get the Dachshund to enter the maze by tossing a tennis ball or a favorite toy inside. Once your dog is confidently entering the dark boxes to look for his ball, you're ready to progress to the next step, the scent trail.

In order to lay a scent trail, you will need live rats or the soiled bedding from rat or mice cages from your local pet shop. If you decide to use bedding instead of a live rat, make rat-bedding tea by soaking the bedding and using the strained liquid to lay a trail in the tunnels.

Of course, nothing compares to the experience of an actual earthdog test with real rats in their cages. Begin with the Introduction to Quarry test to whet your Dachshund's appetite for the rat race.

DACHSHUND FIELD TRIALS

Field trials are, in effect, a form of tracking rather than hunting. Many Dachshund clubs, like Beagle clubs, own their own grounds to run their dogs, and the terrain of these conservancies varies from coast to coast. The quarry for most clubs is cottontail rabbits, though it's not uncommon for jackrabbits to be pursued in the West.

To prepare your Dachshund for a field trial, you must first expose your dog to the scent of a rabbit. Find a place where rabbits are plentiful, such as an open

---

Junior Showmanship

Junior Showmanship classes at dog shows, open to children ages nine to eighteen years old, offer the opportunity for budding fanciers to develop their handling skills and learn about good sportsmanship, dogs, and dog shows. The competitions include handling and performance events, similar to those offered for adults. Judges evaluate the children's handling methods, rather than the animals, although the dogs do need to be registered with the AKC. If your child shows interest in Junior Showmanship, encourage it! Many junior handlers continue in their love of dogs to become professional handlers, veterinarians, breeders, and trainers. Learn more about the Junior Showmanship program at www.akc.org/kids_juniors.

field or a park. Take your Dachshund along at dusk and watch for the rabbits to come out of their holes for suppertime. Watch the path a rabbit takes, and then lead your dog along the path, patting the ground to get him to sniff and track it. Use a short command like "Go find" or "Bunny" to encourage him to begin his search, but don't get him too excited. You don't want your dog to chase the rabbit, just to pick up its scent. Field trial-work isn't fast-paced like agility, so be patient as your dog works out the trail, following the line where the rabbit turned (called a "check"). Once the dog understands what you want him to do, all you need to do is follow wordlessly. In other words, once his nose hits the ground, your mouth closes. Inexperienced dogs will have difficulty keeping their nose to the ground and tracking each check. If your dog starts to excitedly look for the rabbit, calm him down and steer his nose to the ground in the direction where the rabbit took off. Do not interfere with his work once he's back on the line.

The more frequently you give your dog "rabbit time" the better. He will learn quickly if he's exposed to the scents on a regular basis. Daily is best! Once he learns to follow the line over grass, proceed to places where he will have to follow the tracks into the woods or through heavier brush. Exposing your dog to the

Lots of dog in a little package, the Dachshund has potential for great success in many dog sports.

A cuddle with a Doxie friend brings comfort and happiness.

various obstacles he may encounter in a trial, such as logs, streams, ditches, and so forth, will improve his skills negotiating over and around them later.

Visit the AKC website at www.akc.org/events/field_trials/dachshunds to find out more about Dachshund trials and to locate clubs and events near you. Dachshund trials are often held by Beagle field clubs, too. The camaraderie felt among Doxie field people is second to none, so give your Dachshund's nose a chance to do the job it was designed to do.

THERAPY WORK

Dachshunds are universally adored, though not every Dachshund is well suited to become a therapy dog. Therapy dogs—dogs that are trained to visit patients and residents of hospitals, care centers, and senior facilities—must possess sweet, calm temperaments, obey basic commands, and be willing to accept strangers in unfamiliar surroundings.

Some Dachshunds are used in therapy work, visiting nursing homes and hospitals to meet the people there and brighten their days with some licks, cuddles, and head nudges. The breed's convenient size and life-affirming personality make these visits something that patients and residents greatly look forward to.

Not all Doxies fit the therapy dog bill. Many Dachshunds are naturally aloof with strangers and some are wary of children, so owners must devote time to socialize their dogs with a variety of people—young and old alike—and in various situations involving walkers, wheelchairs, hospital equipment, and so forth. If your Doxie has earned the Canine Good Citizen award and is a real people lover, therapy work may be the perfect doggie ministry for you and your dog.

Becoming a therapy dog team involves being trained and certified by one of the many organizations that devote efforts to therapy work. The American Kennel Club itself does not certify therapy dogs, but it works with over fifty organizations that do, including Pet Partners®, Bright and Beautiful Therapy Dogs, Love on a Leash, Therapy Dogs Incorporated (TD Inc.), and Therapy Dogs International (TDI). In 2011, AKC began awarding an AKC Therapy Dog title (THD) to certified therapy dogs that have performed no fewer than fifty therapy visits. Visit the AKC website at www.akc.org/akctherapydog for more information about the program.

Whether you're competing with your Dachshund, making therapy visits, or just playing in the backyard, you're always in for a lot of fun with your personable companion.

At a Glance ...

Keep your Dachshund active by taking him out for at least one or two walks a day. Be careful not to stress his back and legs, and be sure to keep him at a proper weight. Healthy activity will keep the breed's unique frame strong and less vulnerable to injury.

· ·

You and your Dachshund can get involved in a variety of AKC activities, including conformation, obedience, agility, Rally, field trials, tracking, and earthdog events. The sky is the limit for you and your weiner dog.

· ·

Does your Dachshund love meeting new people and clowning around? If you want to share your Dachshund's sweet antics with the community, consider therapy dog work. Your personable Doxie may be just what the doctor ordered to give a dose of cheer to those in hospitals, nursing homes, and other similar facilities.

Resources

BOOKS

The American Kennel Club's Meet the Breeds: Dog Breeds from A to Z, 2012 edition (Irvine, California: I-5 Press, 2011) The ideal puppy buyer's guide, this book has all you need to know about each breed currently recognized by the AKC.

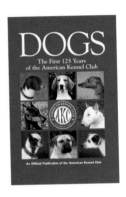

The Complete Dog Book, 20th edition (New York: Ballantine Books, 2006) This official publication of the AKC, first published in 1929, includes the complete histories and breed standards of 153 recognized breeds, as well as information on general care and the dog sport.

The Complete Dog Book for Kids (New York: Howell Book House, 1996) Specifically geared toward young people, this official publication of the AKC presents 149 breeds and varieties, as well as introductory owners' information.

Citizen Canine: Ten Essential Skills Every Well-Mannered Dog Should Know by Mary R. Burch, PhD (Freehold, New Jersey: Kennel Club Books, 2010) This official AKC publication is the definitive guide to the AKC's Canine Good Citizen® Program, recognized as the gold standard of behavior for dogs, with more than half a million dogs trained.

DOGS: The First 125 Years of the American Kennel Club (Freehold, New Jersey: Kennel Club Books, 2009) This official AKC publication presents an authoritative, complete history of the AKC, including detailed information not found in any other volume.

Dog Heroes of September 11th: A Tribute to America's Search and Rescue Dogs, 10th anniversary edition, by Nona Kilgore Bauer (Freehold, New Jersey: Kennel Club Books, 2011) A publication to salute the canines that served in the recovery missions following the September 11th attacks, this book serves as a lasting tribute to these noble American heroes.

The Original Dog Bible: The Definitive Source for All Things Dog, 2nd edition, by Kristin Mehus-Roe (Irvine, California: I-5 Press, 2009) This 831-page magnum opus includes more than 250 breed profiles, hundreds of color photographs, and a wealth of information on every dog topic imaginable—thousands of practical tips on grooming, training, care, and much more.

PERIODICALS

American Kennel Club Gazette

Every month since 1889, serious dog fanciers have looked to the *AKC Gazette* for authoritative advice on training, showing, breeding, and canine health. Each issue includes the breed columns section, written by experts from the respective breed clubs. Only available electronically.

AKC Family Dog

This is a bimonthly magazine for the dog lover whose special dog is "just a pet." Helpful tips, how-tos, and features are written in an entertaining and reader-friendly format. It's a lifestyle magazine for today's busy families who want to enjoy a rewarding, mutually happy relationship with their canine companions.

Dog Fancy

The world's most widely read dog magazine, *Dog Fancy* celebrates dogs and the people who love them. Each monthly issue includes info on cutting-edge medical developments, health and fitness (with a focus on prevention,

treatment, and natural therapy), behavior and training, travel and activities, breed profiles and dog news, issues and trends for purebred and mixed-breed dog owners. The magazine informs, inspires, and entertains while promoting responsible dog ownership. Throughout its more than forty-year history, *Dog Fancy* has garnered numerous honors, including being named the Best All-Breed Magazine by the Dog Writers Association of America.

Dogs in Review

For more than fifteen years, *Dogs in Review* has showcased the finest dogs in the United States and from around the world. The emphasis has always been on strong content, with input

from distinguished breeders, judges, and handlers worldwide. This global perspective distinguishes this monthly publication from its competitors—no other North American dog-show magazine gathers together so many international experts to enlighten and entertain its readership.

Dog World Annual

Dog World (formerly *Dogs USA*) is an annual lifestyle magazine published by the editors of *Dog Fancy* that covers all aspects of the dog world: culture, art, history, travel, sports, and science. It also profiles breeds to help prospective owners choose the best dogs for their future needs, such as a potential show champion, super service dog, great pet, or competitive star.

Natural Dog

Natural Dog is the magazine dedicated to giving a dog a natural lifestyle. From nutritional choices to grooming to dog-supply options, this publication helps readers make the transition from traditional to natural methods. The magazine also explores the array of complementary treatments available for today's dogs: acupuncture, massage, homeopathy, aromatherapy, and much

Puppies USA

Also from the editors of *Dog Fancy*, this annual magazine offers essential information for all new puppy owners. *Puppies USA* is lively and informative, including advice on general care, nutrition, grooming, and training techniques for all puppies, whether purebred or mixed breed, adopted, rescued, or purchased. In addition, it offers family fun through quizzes, contests, and much more. An extensive breeder directory is included.

WEBSITES

www.akc.org

The American Kennel Club (AKC) website is an excellent starting point for researching dog breeds and learning about puppy care. The site lists hundreds of breeders, along with basic information about breed selection and basic care. The site also has links to the national breed club of every AKC-recognized breed; breed-club sites offer plenty of detailed breed information, as well as lists of member breeders. In addition, you can find the AKC National Breed Club Rescue List at www.akc.org/breeds/rescue.cfm. If looking for purebred puppies, go to www.puppybuyerinfo.com for AKC classifieds and parent-club referrals.

www.dogchannel.com

Powered by *Dog Fancy*, Dog Channel is "the website for dog lovers," where hundreds of thousands of visitors each month find extensive information on breeds, training, health and nutrition, puppies, care, activities, and more. Interactive features include forums, Dog College, games, and Club Dog, a free club where dog lovers can create blogs for their pets and earn points to buy products. Dog Channel is the one-stop site for all things dog.

www.meetthebreeds.com

The official website of the AKC Meet the Breeds® event, hosted by the American Kennel Club in the Jacob Javits Center in New York City in the fall. The first Meet the Breeds event took place in 2009. The website includes information on every recognized breed of dog and cat, alphabetically listed, as well as the breeders, demonstration facilitators, sponsors, and vendors participating in the annual event.

AKC AFFILIATES

The **AKC Museum of the Dog**, established in 1981, is located in St. Louis, Missouri, and houses the world's finest collection of art devoted to the dog. Visit www.museumofthedog.org.

The **AKC Humane Fund** promotes the joy and value of responsible and productive pet ownership through education, outreach, and grant-making. Monies raised may fund grants to organizations that teach responsible pet ownership; provide for the health and well-being of all dogs; and preserve and celebrate the human-animal bond and the evolutionary relationship between dogs and humankind. Go to www.akchumanefund.org.

The **American Kennel Club Companion Animal Recovery (CAR) Corporation** is dedicated to reuniting lost microchipped and tattooed pets with their owners. AKC CAR maintains a permanent-identification database and provides lifetime recovery services 24 hours a day, 365 days a year, for all animal species. Millions of pets are enrolled in the program, which was established in 1995. Visit www.akccar.org.

The **American Kennel Club Canine Health Foundation (AKC CHF), Inc.** is the largest foundation in the world to fund canine-only health studies for purebred and mixed-breed dogs. More than $22 million has been allocated in research funds to more than 500 health studies conducted to help dogs live longer, healthier lives. Go to www.akcchf.org.

AKC PROGRAMS

The **Canine Good Citizen Program (CGC)** was established in 1989 and is designed to recognize dogs that have good manners at home and in the community. This rapidly growing, nationally recognized program stresses responsible dog ownership for owners and basic training and good manners for dogs. All dogs that pass the ten-step Canine Good Citizen test receive a certificate from the American Kennel Club. Go to www.akc.org/events/cgc.

The **AKC S.T.A.R. Puppy Program** is designed to get dog owners and their puppies off to a good start and is aimed at loving dog owners who have taken the time to attend basic obedience classes with their puppies. After completing a six-week training course, the puppy must pass the AKC S.T.A.R. Puppy test, which evaluates Socialization, Training, Activity, and Responsibility. Go to www.akc.org/starpuppy.

The **AKC Therapy Dog** program recognizes all American Kennel Club dogs and their owners who have given their time and helped people by volunteering as a therapy dog-and-owner team. The AKC Therapy Dog program is an official American Kennel Club title awarded to dogs that have worked to improve the lives of the people they have visited. The AKC Therapy Dog title (AKC ThD) can be earned by dogs that have been certified by recognized therapy dog organizations. For more information, visit www.akc.org/akctherapydog.

Index

AMERICAN KENNEL CLUB®

Advocating for the purebred dog as a family companion, advancing canine health and well-being, working to protect the rights of all dog owners and promoting responsible dog ownership, the **American Kennel Club:**

Sponsors more than **22,000 sanctioned events** annually including conformation, agility, obedience, rally, tracking, lure coursing, earthdog, herding, field trial, hunt test, and coonhound events

Features a **10-step Canine Good Citizen® program** that rewards dogs who have good manners at home and in the community

Has reunited more than **400,000** lost pets with their owners through the AKC Companion Animal Recovery - visit **www.akccar.org**

Created and supports the AKC Canine Health Foundation, which funds research projects using the more than **$22 million** the AKC has donated since 1995 - visit **www.akcchf.org**

Joins **animal lovers** through education, outreach and grant-making via the AKC Humane Fund - visit **www.akchumanefund.org**

We're more than champion dogs. We're the dog's champion.

www.akc.org